Neil Clark lived first 20 years of life in Notting Dale, North Kensington worked in public libraries for 10 years. Then as a management trainer and consultant, he lived and worked in Dudley, Horsham, Bexley Heath and Broadstairs. Married with three children. He has previously published five books.

This was the beginning

Neil Clark

For Lewis Ashman, my oldest friend

Neil Clark

A Lost Childhood

AUSTIN MACAULEY PUBLISHERS™
LONDON * CAMBRIDGE * NEW YORK * SHARJAH

A CIP catalogue record for this title is available from the British Library.

ISBN 9781398494961 (Paperback)
ISBN 9781398494978 (ePub e-book)

www.austinmacauley.com

First Published 2022
Austin Macauley Publishers Ltd®
1 Canada Square
Canary Wharf
London
E14 5AA

Table of Contents

Preface

That great humourist, Damon Runyon, once observed that 'I came to the conclusion long ago that all life is six to five against.

Sometimes those odds can be improved.

January 2022, Broadstairs

1
The Way It Was

I was born in 1947, one of the baby boomers, and the world was so different then; behaviours and attitudes more closely resembled those of the First World War than they do in 2020.When I tried to explain quotidian experiences to my children, they were incredulous, suspecting me of exaggeration if not complete falsehood, but that is the way it was.

We grew up surrounded by the legacies of World War II. Until the 1960s, at least in London, bombsites were an accepted part of the background. Children used them as alternative playgrounds, teenagers as venues for gang fights. In Notting Dale, where I grew up, many of the buildings that remained upright were equally bad. The ones not scarred with war damage exhibited stains of neglect and the drabness of poverty. This was an area that had been based on impoverishment. For me, life was black and white with large areas of grey, and dust seemed to cover everything. No one complained, a dreary misery seemed to be an accepted part of life. As a child I knew no different.

For all but a short interval I lived the first twenty years of my life in a two-bedroomed council flat, 5 Moreland

House, in Lancaster Road. There was no central heating. When we moved in, there was a leaded grange in the front room, which was great for baking potatoes but was useless for heating purposes. In 1958, the council converted this into an open fire with a back boiler. This meant we had hot water whenever the fire was lit, which was mainly the hard winter months. In my bedroom there was a small open basket fire about the size of a handbag. When lit, which was rare, it provided more light than heat. In my mother's bedroom, which she shared with my sister, there was a small gas fire which did provide some heat. The only room guaranteed to be warm was the kitchen which was at the other end of the flat. The heat came from the gas rings which were turned on first thing in the morning. All this meant that winters were extraordinarily cold experiences, and that keeping warm was a full-time occupation. I can still remember the bitterly cold winter of 1962–3 when snow lay on the ground for weeks and the football season was suspended. Even when our fires were at full blast – which indeed was rare – to keep warm meant sitting within the five-feet radiated boundary of the open fire. As soon as you crossed the barrier the cold would claim you. Going to the toilet was a polar expedition. Because of this reliance on radiated heat, it was a common sight to see women with strangely mottled-coloured legs complaining of chilblains.

To prepare to go to bed meant undressing in front of a fire then scooting into the bedroom, shivering in bed until body heat warmed the icy sheets. On bitterly cold nights it was advisable to put coats on top of the bedclothes. However, even with these additions getting up in the morning was even worse. Without the benefits of double-glazing ice would form on the inside of windows, and cold winds would rattle the old sash cords so that the first thing you saw in the morning were breath clouds. Leaping out of bed and running to the kitchen was always an act of courage.

To make matters worse getting fuel was always a problem. In the years before 1958 coal was rationed, Londoners had to collect coal from designated sites. When coal was not available, we used coke – a dreadful fuel that was a blue-grey object with the texture of an aero bar that glowed rather than burned when lit. They only way to receive heat from a coke fire was to lay on top of the fire. Even then the other side of your body would remain cold. The only places with central heating, often antiquated and inadequate, were schools and libraries. Even there I could remember keeping a coat on.

We only had running hot water when the boiler was heated by the front room fire. In summer, washing yourself or washing your hair meant heating up pans of water and taking over the kitchen to undertake a strip wash. If my nasal memories are correct, then I am clear that not everybody would put themselves to the trouble. This was also at a time when deodorants were rarely used, particularly by men. This meant that travel on public transport for children, particularly, was a real ordeal. Standing on a crowded tube at arm pit level did induce major nausea. It was certainly not uncommon to see men walking around with huge sweat patches on their shirts the size of Asia. Women used special shields in their dresses which hid the stains but did little about the smells.

There was a big fuss when sweets came off the ration in 1953 but few people remember that food restrictions lasted a further year. The age of austerity meant that most homes, particularly the ones I visited, simply did not have food available. Shopping took place each day, and the big shop on Saturday merely lasted two days. It had to because nothing could be bought on a Sunday. For a hungry child, and I seemed to spend most of my childhood in a state of hunger, there was nothing to eat outside the three basic meals. Like many other families we only had a larder in which were kept some basic foodstuffs – tea, instant coffee, butter, milk, and the bowl of lard used for the fry up and spreading on sandwiches. Our larder was simply a cupboard in the kitchen adjacent to an outside wall with a vent just below ceiling height. For breakfast we had cornflakes. The main meal – usually at lunch time – was a variation of meat and two veg. This could be sausages, gammon, shepherds or cottage pie, liver and bacon, kidneys, but very rarely, a joint of meat or chicken. Vegetables would be boiled to mush on a gas ring. This would be followed by a jam sponge pudding or spotted dick with custard. In summer, this would be replaced by a tin of fruit or a jelly with Carnation milk for flavour. The evening tea would be sandwiches or beans on toast. The variation would be tinned spaghetti on toast. In between these meals – nothing.

Even when sweets came off the ration a child would be lucky to receive one bar of chocolate and a bag of crisps each week if they lived in my neighbourhood. I grew up believing that food was not a pleasure, but a fuel to keep you going. My mother, like many, simply had no interest in food or cooking. When I started part-time work in the evening, I would return a couple of hours after dinner to find my meal between two plates simmering over a boiling pan of water.

My first task was to break the congealed gravy seal that cemented the two plates together. Not surprisingly, much of my late dinners were scraped into the bin. I grew up totally unaware that food had tastes and could be enjoyed.

School meals, which were immeasurably better than my mother's cooking, provided for most children the basic form of nourishment. However, for me there was a major penalty clause with these meals in the form of various milk puddings – rice with scabrous skin, semolina, and horror of horrors, tapioca or frog's eyes. The most sadistic teachers were those who made you eat up everything before you left the table. The kind ones simply understood what suffering was and turned a blind eye. Like other kids on free school meals, I used to attend special schools open in the summer holidays that provided us with a lunch as well as some play activity. Although the stigma attached to having free school meals grew more acute over time, I cannot imagine how I would have survived without this service.

The only food treats in my childhood were fish and chips or pie and mash. Because of cost these were rare luxuries but sixty years later I still enjoy, when I can, entering the marble pleasure palaces that offered a pie swimming in green liquor. However, even austerity had some benefits because there was little incidence of obesity. During my school life we averaged one fat boy in a class of thirty plus.

Although the NHS was up and running the quality of dentistry was basic. The hours that I spent in a chair having fillings or extractions were tedious and unsatisfactory. That I have reached the age of 74 without dentures is a testimony to later dentists who have spent long hours on remedial attention.

Although clothes rationing ended in 1949, my memories of childhood were that they remained in limited supply long afterwards. Whether this was due to availability or cost it was difficult to determine. I do know that a couple of drawers and a few hooks was more than sufficient to contain my wardrobe, and I suspect, most other people. Certainly, as a teenager I had a set of school clothes, an overcoat or mackintosh, two pairs of shoes. As a child, all I can remember was that men wore shirts that were white, blue or grey. Sometime in the late 1950s striped shirts began to make an appearance, but it was only in the early 1960s that colours and casual clothes began to appear in a big way. Until then, in summer, men's casual style was limited to shirt collars being opened and spread flat across the sports jacket. The truly daring male also wore open sandals with the fustian black socks. I can remember dads sitting on deck chairs in mid-summer with their jackets on, and the obligatory knotted handkerchief on their head. Colour was more available in women's clothing, but they tended to be of the pastel variety, and consisted of huge flower patterns. There was no teenage clothing at all; you were either a child or an adult, and dressed accordingly.

Many of our clothes were bought from tallymen. These were men who used to carry small collection of clothes in the back of their small A7 vans and deliver them to your door. Not only was the choice restricted but the quality was also poor. However, this meant that families like mine would buy clothes on credit and pay back an inflated sum over many weeks. The real killer with this system is that once you started then the debts began to mount very quickly. The alternative was to buy on credit clothing 'cheques'

(Provident and Bradford were the ones I remember) which could only be redeemed at certain shops. Their standard of clothing was as poor as the tallymen. In my family, aunts and uncles would buy one of the cheques say for £30 as a Christmas present for six or seven members of the family. If you were not top of the list – as I was not in my family – then your £2–3 gift could only be spent long after the holidays were over. That was assuming that no one else spent your share.

I lived at a time, and in an area, of great privation, without being aware of doing so. Poverty is truly relative, and only becomes apparent when you can see that others live a different life. Some days we did not eat a meal but bread and dripping. We were housed, clothed and fed, however poorly, but the same seemed to be true of everyone I knew. We did not get a TV until 1958, although one of my aunts had one, and one of my school friends used to let me watch episodes of *The Lone Ranger* on his set. Being without TV never seemed to be a hardship, particularly as the wireless provided such entertainment. I feel privileged to have grown up listening to programmes as rewarding as, *Journey into Space*, *Take it from Here*, *Beyond our Ken*, *Hancock's Half Hour*, *Educating Archie*, plus the whole range of Children's Hour. Not only were they entertaining but you had to use your imagination to form the pictures.

Similarly, we had no fridge, hoover, washing machine, or telephone during the whole of my childhood, and the black metal irons we used to press our clothes had to be heated on a gas ring. This meant making do and mending. For example, keeping butter and milk in bowls of water in the larder during warm spells to stop them turning rancid;

washing clothes and sheets in the bath; hanging dripping wet clothes on rails in the bathroom; and, trying to avoid scorch marks on white shirts. In comparison with people in our country who are living in poverty now the benchmarks are completely different, albeit the sense of squalor remains. There is no inherent virtue in being poor. It does not build character or provide an impetus to betterment. It simply means that daily life is grim, tiring and dispiriting. As a child I held no stupid idea that life would get better. Largely because I did not know what better looked like.

The only person I knew with a motor vehicle, a van, was my uncle Bill, who was a general dealer, and used his vehicle primarily for business reasons. It would be my late teens before I was a passenger in a car. As to believing that I would ever own one that was entering the realms of complete fantasy. Life without a car was no hardship in London. If you wanted to travel, there was always public transport or walking. I ended up doing a lot of walking. Mind you, there was little reason to go travelling. Most children stayed within the boundaries of their London 'village'.

Although kids lacked food, heat and decent clothes, we did have the freedom of the streets to play. During school holidays, once I had done my share of the housework, I could be on the streets until the late evening. I might play cricket in the morning at the designated open school and then eat my lunch, but the rest of the time was my own. In our flats there was a play area, and it was not unusual for a seven-hour game of cricket or football to keep us occupied. However, on Sundays we were not allowed to use the facility. The caretaker would take the bats and balls of children who dared to break this injunction.

Other kids might be lucky enough to live in designated play streets, which meant that road traffic was not allowed to use them during specified hours. Instead, kids played all day outside their front doors, while on summer evening their mothers would gather on the steps to exchange news and gossip. The public balconies of our flats provided the same service.

We would also use parks and recreation centres without any kind of supervision. It is quite extraordinary now with all the worry and concern about paedophiles that we were allowed such freedom. At most parks I played in there would be at least one known pervert sitting on his own watching the kids play. Whatever the weather they would sit with macs spread across their loins. We all knew what they were and what they would do and had our own ways of seeing them off. If name calling and laughter did not work, then a well-directed football or cricket ball sent out the message. Quite clearly children were being abused then, as now, but I think that our safety was not based on ignorance or innocence but on communal safeguarding. We looked after ourselves and each other because adults lived in another and different world.

I cannot remember the time that I first became aware of sex but certainly by the age of eleven not only did I know about the paedophiles, gays, lesbians, transsexuals, prostitutes and cross dressers, but I knew them as people and lived among them. Some of my middle-class contemporaries have told me that they did not discover the notion of homosexuality until in their late teens, but in our area such knowledge was simply part of the survival kit.

During the 1950s our parents, not for any religious reasons, would ensure that we attended Sunday school. The major purpose of this command was to ensure that they would have a couple of hours every Sunday to put their feet up. Attendance at the Sunday school often led on to joining the guides or scouts, or, in my case the Lifeboys, the junior version of the Boys Brigade. I was not attracted by the uniform – a sailor's hat, blue roll neck jumper with pennants on the shoulder. The evening activities that they organised were a great attraction from the utter boredom that prevailed. However, when it came to boredom – particularly of the terminal kind – then Sundays were in a class of their own. To appreciate what this felt like then just listen to the Tony Hancock radio episode, *Sunday afternoon at home*. The one certainty for Sunday was that everything closed.

However, the Lifeboys, was only a period of transition. The real-life saver for me was turning eleven and being able to join a Boys' Club which I describe at great length later. This provided not just an escape from boredom but one of the supreme pleasures of my childhood.

However, life was not always about play. From the age of ten, I, like many of my friends looked for part-time jobs. From that age onwards, I did paper rounds, worked in a tyre and battery shop, then a butchers, sold lemons off a stall in Portobello market, worked late evenings (hence the spoiled dinners) and Saturdays in a public library, and became a 'totter', like '*Steptoe and Son*'. This involved two of us hiring for the day a pushcart and going around the streets calling, 'Old rags, bone, lumber', and, more productively rooting in the dustbins of houses around Holland Park and Kensington. In this capacity I was apprentice to an experienced 'totter' a few years older than me. We hardly made much money but at least we tried. Pocket money was very much a middle-class notion; if we wanted money, we had to earn our own.

Many people of my generation have looked back on this period as a time of great pleasure and certainty – before the permissive 1960s turned the world upside down. However, I do not share that rosy view. There were benefits to living then, and I have tried to list the ones that meant much to me. But I was equally aware of the down sides.

For this was a foreign country based on authority. This was most obvious in the continuing practice of both capital and corporal punishment. But daily life saw an oppressive discipline rule all our lives. Children were routinely beaten not only by parents and teachers, but most adults took it upon themselves to physically chastise what they perceived as naughty behaviour in public places. The cliché of a policeman clipping a youngster around the ear may seem terribly worthy now but at the time it was a punishment which allowed the victim no redress or even any notion of justice. As children it often felt as if we were at the mercy of an adult world that would not listen. When an adult made a judgment, the child had to accept – even when it was patently unjust or incorrect. Everyone in society had their place, and whatever level you occupied you had the right to expect the people below you to defer to your view. And the lowest level in the hierarchy were children. This atmosphere bred many who took on authority at many levels, and the term 'juvenile delinquent' had great currency in the late

1950s. As did the term ‘generation gap’. Attempts to communicate or make contact across the divide between adults and children was extraordinarily difficult. Childhood seemed to be a penance that needed to be served before you earnt the right to oppress your own children.

Equally, this was a time of rampant racism and sexism. Black people were treated with open aggression and violence. Gays were ostracised and persecuted. Bad language was heard on every street but generally not from women. Women had to follow strict rules of behaviour – not be loud, or contradict men (certainly not in public), not to smoke on the streets or go into pubs. If they stepped out of line, there were punishments. Like children, women should be seen but not heard. In some ways the Victorian age persisted into the new Elizabethan age. Which brings me to my grandfather and the beginning of my story.

2
Grandfather

My family starts with my grandfather. His influence on subsequent generations has been immense, but I suspect it has also been sadly misrepresented. My own memories of him are meagre but powerful. He died two months shy of his 68th birthday, although physically he looked at least ten to fifteen years older, and his heavy drinking had affected both his body and mind. I was just over six years old when he died on 12 June 1953 and can only recall his last six months with some degree of clarity.

I have vivid memories of sitting on his lap and lying against his chest, feeling the rough stubble of his chin and the soft silkiness of the white scarf that was tucked into his double-breasted jacket. I felt both comforted and cared for by him, a totally unique experience in my childhood, one that has carried over the years. The smell of camp coffee and condensed milk, a deadly combination for health purposes, brings him back vividly. Many years later I saw Robin Bailey play Uncle Mort in *I Didn't Know You Cared* on television, and it was like my grandfather had returned. Though this one spoke and moved on the television. My grandfather of memory was always silent and had the kind of ugly face that gave character to French film stars, and in its own way made them handsome.

He lived about a five-minute walk from our flat in Moreland House and was a frequent visitor. I would also go to his first floor flat in a little terrace house and take back the empty cordial bottles to the newsagent. I do not remember who kept the pennies for their return, me or him. He had been warned off alcohol by his doctor and had got into the habit of drinking vast quantities of soft drinks as some sort of recompense. Unfortunately, his conversion came too late. His physical and mental decline increased when he went on the wagon. One morning at 2:00 a.m. he knocked at our door with a plate in one hand, his knife and fork in another, asking for his dinner. He needed some persuasion that he was mistaken as to the time of day. In the last months of his life, he became housebound, and then latterly, bedbound, spending time in such a deep sleep that he appeared comatose. When he got to this stage, I was forbidden from seeing him.

One of the stories later told to me was that one Sunday morning he awoke, went to the door of his first-floor flat and shouted down the stairs at what he imagined to be me. He believed that I was making fun of him and cried at my cruelty. The fact that he was in tears was incredible. His neighbour, having watched the performance, saw him back to bed. Just after this, his eldest daughter, Lizzie, on death watch by his bedside, was shocked to see him rise up in the bed. He screamed at her to get out of his house. The story was that she had been discovered going through his drawers looking for money and trinkets. She was actively managing her inheritance, a habit she brought to many death beds. She screamed and fled the house. The irony of the event was that she had only agreed to the death watch because she believed that he was in a coma. That close to death he still had the ability to frighten his children.

So, why do I have fond memories of this formidable man? Although he disliked, even seemed to hate, all his five children, he appeared to be very fond of me. Whether it was because I was illegitimate, or because my aunts and uncles hated me for the shame, they said that I brought to the family, I do not know. Perhaps, he was just perverse and decided to like me to upset them. I hope that he just liked me. He was the nearest I got to care in my childhood. I grew to understand why he disliked his surviving children. It was a point of view easy to acquire.

He was born Albert Osborne, the eldest of three boys on 15 August 1885, at Hope Avenue, Kingston on Thames. His father, Edward, was a fishmonger, and his mother, Alice, formerly Lee, was listed as a laundress on his birth certificate. They had two more boys and allegedly some girls, though I have found no details of the latter. Ted was born two years later, and Henry in 1889. After my grandfather's death Ted introduced himself to my mother. She did not appear to know anything about her uncle though she had been brought up less than a mile from where he lived. Ted lived a street away from Granddad's last address and owned a general dealer's shop. According to Ted an argument led to a street fight before the Second World War, and they had not spoken to each other since. If they met in the street, said Ted, they would simply ignore each other. To my eyes, Ted seemed kind and considerate, but he was obviously as stubborn and fiery as my granddad. They were hard times as lived by hard people.

Granddad married Elizabeth Judd on 18 April 1911 at St Clements Church in the parish of Kensington. The home address on their wedding certificate was 13 Hunt Street, North Kensington. All their five children were born at this address; Elizabeth on 16 November 1912; Nellie one year later, Albert in 1919, Ivy in 1923, and lastly, my mother, Alice, in 1926.

The family suffered a lot of illness. This was no great surprise for the period and that part of London. Ivy and Alice contacted rheumatic fever and were sent away to a special school in the country for some years. Nellie caught TB and died aged 24 in April 1938. Her mother died six months later of the same disease. At which point, allegedly, Granddad called at the school for Ivy and Alice and said, "Your mother is dead, you are coming home for the funeral, and I don't won't anyone crying and showing me up."

Although my mother told me this story in terrible tones, citing this as an example of his deplorable behaviour, it became a precedent that she would later follow. My mother always spoke well of Nellie and her own mother but the only evidence she adduced of their goodness was of being taken to the public library by Nellie. Whether they were substantially different from the rest of the family, or, whether their characters were improved by death I have no idea. I would hope for her sake that for once she was not romanticising about her past.

My grandmother died in a sanatorium but, allegedly, was planning to leave her husband just before her death. One of the reasons for her prospective separation was that Granddad had thrown his son, Albert, out of the house at the age of 15, and he had then gone to live with the family of a doctor. Again, I have no evidence for any of this, apart from my mother's words, but it certainly fitted with the general image of Granddad as a strict Victorian paterfamilias whose word and wishes were law. He clearly terrified all members of his family, and everyone learned to keep away from him. Whatever the reality, his children seemed to have emerged severely damaged from their childhood and then inflicted suffering on their own families.

I am quite cautious about accepting that Granddad was totally to blame for all that happened. One of the reasons being that some of the stories about him I even questioned as a child. For example, my mother insisted that her dad was a Gypsy and had first lived in a house when he married. She proposed this on the basis that his mother's maiden name was Lee (A well-known Gypsy name). The simple evidence that the birth certificates for Granddad and his brothers all contained house addresses in Kingston on Thames was never seen to throw doubt on her argument. I was also told that Granddad met his wife when she was a laundress at Osborne House. The fact that there was no evidence that either had visited the Isle of Wight seemed incidental to this claim. When I read on his birth certificate that his mother's occupation was that of laundress, I simply assumed that this occupation had been transposed onto his wife.

I was also told, not just by my mother but by Lizzie, that Granddad served in the Indian army as a boy, and that he fought the boxer Bombardier Billie Wells. His only known military record showed that he enlisted in 1914 and served solely on the western front. So, his army career in India seems as mythical as that of his visit to the Isle of Wight. Similarly, although their dates overlapped, there is no evidence, or indeed, any likely opportunity when a boxing match with Billy Wells could have taken place. Granddad was certainly a street fighter, but I suspect that most of the fights took place on Wormwood Scrubs on a Sunday morning. This was the local spot in Notting Dale for settling issues.

An amateur genealogist once told me that many families develop myths about their forebears and are most resistant to them being questioned. When I raised questions about these stories, I was told that I had no right to even ask the questions. Many years later I started to collect copies of birth and death certificates, and when I showed the evidence to her, my mother blamed her eldest sister for keeping her in the dark. The family simply did not ask questions of each other and showed no real interest outside their daily activities. Near the end of her own life my mother complained that she knew nothing about the life or her own mother. By then she was the last living child of her parents.

What is certain, however, is that Granddad enlisted on 3 September 1914 in the Middlesex Regiment but served in the 11th (Service) Battalion of the Royal Fusiliers. This was a battalion of the new armies formed at Hounslow on 6 September 1914, and came under the command of the 54th Brigade, 18th (Eastern) Division. The battalion was moved to Colchester, and then in May 1915 moved to Salisbury Plain. The battalion landed at Boulogne in July 1915.

Although his own Army records were lost in the Second World War, I was able to discover from the official records that the 11th Battalion was involved in several actions on the Western Front, including:

1916	Battles at Albert, Bazentin Ridge, Delville Wood, Thiepval Ridge, Ancre Heights, capture of Regina Trench Ancre.
1917	Operations on the Ancre, German retreat to the Hindenburg Line, Third Battle of the Scarpe, Battle of Pilkern Ridge, Battle of Langemarck, First and Second Battles of Paschaendale.
1918	Battle of San Quentin, Battle of Avre, actions at Viliers-Brettoneux, Battle of Albert, captured the Tara and Usna hills, second Battle of Bapaume, the Battle of Epehy, Battle of San Quentin canal, battle of the Selle, Battle of Sambre.

The 11th Battalion ended the war near Le Cateau.

Granddad's regimental number was 7383 and he remained a Private throughout the War. He was discharged on 22 February 1919 and transferred to the Army Reserve on 28 March 1919. His certificate of Demobilisation stated against 'Medals and Decorations section' the simple statement 'Nil'. Apparently, this meant that he was awarded 'Pip, Squeak and Wilfred' the British War Medal, the British Victory Medal, and the 1914–15 Star. His 'Certificate of Employment During the War' stated against 'Military Qualifications' that he had achieved 'Musketry Class 1'.

Although it is unlikely that he served in all the above actions involving the Battalion Granddad spent four years on the western front in some of the worst battles. To have survived these experiences was remarkable, for his family not to have any stories to pass on about his experiences is in some ways more remarkable. I know that WW1 veterans were notoriously tight-lipped about the war but clearly none of his family in any way gave him any credit for his service or took pride in his achievements.

Whatever his character was before the War it is likely that the impact of these experiences would have been profound. Service personnel then were left to their own resources to come to terms with the horrors, and either repressed them or simply kept them quiet. The veterans that I met as a child were all very private and secretive about their war experiences. Typical of the ones I knew, was a neighbour in Talbot House, a block of flats at the back of Moreland House. I tried to talk to him about his experiences, but he always brushed off any questions with a smile and a change of topic. Having since read extensively about what they went through I am not surprised. The following is about my memory of this man.

The Veteran of Wwi

He hid his life inside a biscuit tin
Behind a picture on the kitchen shelf,
His medals and some papers lay within
Which he would let me look at by myself.
Each Spring and Summer he would take a chair
Outside his flat to watch the evening die.
He loved to feel the wind upon his hair,

Would say, "It was an angel passing by."
And I, a young boy, being open to such things,
Learnt about angels and the power of their wings.

We have become so used to the concept of post-traumatic stress and the various treatments available for service personnel and others, that it is easy to forget that his generation just went back home and got on with the business of living. One can only imagine the transition to normal civilian life and how it affected the servicemen and their families. I only wished that I had the opportunity to talk to Granddad about his war experiences. I would have persisted until he gave in.

I have made several trips to the WW1 battlefields and paid homage to his service.

After the war, Granddad was a flower seller and I have in my possession a remarkable picture of him in the 1930s when he is both dressed in, and carrying, flowers to celebrate some royal event, probably the Coronation of George VI. The only other picture I have of him is taken before the First World War, a studio portrait with either Lizzie or Nellie sitting on his knee. Although it is a studio portrait and he looks steadily into the camera with the baby poised on his knee, it is interesting to me that he chose such a paternal subject. It does not quite fit with someone who reputedly hated all his children. Perhaps he did, and this is purely for show. Or perhaps, he changed dramatically after 1919. The following picture, however, leaves the question open.

My grandfather c1912

Grandad, the flower seller c1936

During the Second World War he volunteered for and served in the London Heavy Rescue Service from 1939 to 1945, digging people and bodies out of the rubble. He received a letter from the London County Council dated December 1945 expressing their appreciation of his service. He was aged 54 when he volunteered for this onerous duty.

I accept the probability of his tyrannical behaviour to his children. But no one gave him any recognition for his ten years' service to his country and what that might have cost him mentally. I am also ready to admit my bias for an old man that sat me on his knee and let me stroke his face. For that experience alone, I am more than willing to remember him with affection. In contrast my mother never held me, kissed me, or even told me that she loved me. I think I deserve to hang on to the memory of my granddad.

My grandfather died on 12 June 1953. I was not allowed to attend the funeral but can remember being at Lizzie's house on the day he was buried in Gunnersbury cemetery.

3
The Osborne Family

Granddad's eldest daughter, Lizzie, married in the 1930s to Joe, and had three children, Joe, John and Linda. For a short period, just after his National Service in the 1950s, I got to know the eldest son, Joe, in the only way that a young boy could get to know someone ten years older; through hero worship. Joe was a goalkeeper for Hayes FC in the late 1950s, and he used to take me with him to attend home and away matches. It only lasted for one season, but it was a great privilege. Each match started with a green line journey from Holland Park, and sometimes ended, with me enjoying an evening meal with the players. Joe then married into a prosperous family of greengrocers. This was a marriage that put stars in the eyes of Lizzie. From that point onwards she would do anything and everything for her daughter-in-law and her family. Joe, and his wife, Sheila, became tenants of a pub in Maida Vale, and seemed to have a good future in front of them. Although they had a daughter the marriage slowly fell apart. Sheila, like the rest of her family was a hard worker and I think she considered that Joe did not pull his weight. During this period of decline Lizzie sided with Sheila and her granddaughter, even though her son ended up in hospital suffering from stress. She remained absolutely besotted with her grandchild and her in-laws. That was the nearest she ever got, I suspect, to expressing affection for anyone.

For two years, the younger son, John, became like a big brother to me. There was only a six-year gap in our ages, and I consciously tried to follow in his footsteps, including joining the Harrow Boys Club. Unfortunately, John continued the family tradition of a bad marriage, though in his case it was obvious from the start. The sadness was that before the marriage in 1962 he consulted with me as to whether he should marry the woman he had got pregnant. Although this may speak well of our relationship it now strikes me as an awfully sad event for John that I was the only family member he felt able to speak to. At the age of fifteen I warned him not to marry, but he ignored my advice. He felt that he had to do the right thing by the woman. Lizzie took against his wife, and then their daughter. For her, they provided a stark contrast with Joe's in-laws. Lizzie would use Christmas and birthdays as a public means of reward and punishment to her two granddaughters. One would have an expensive present while the other had a cheap one or was completely ignored. This was one of her well-honed tactics, and not surprisingly drove John and his family away from her and his family. There was some form of reconciliation when his mother died, but essentially John went his own way. I did meet him at the hospital bedside of my mother around about 2006. We spoke briefly and superficially about the past. It was too long a gap, and, I had no desire to look for ways to bridge it. Sometimes moving on is the only option.

Linda, Lizzie's youngest child, was three weeks younger than me, and passed out of my life 50 years ago. Our only relationship was minimal and really centred on Lizzie's tactic of favouritism. Each year my birthday would be forgotten or remembered late, whereas Linda's would be publicly recognised. Lizzie had all the predictability of a metronome, and the annual repetition was boring. I only reacted badly once to her over this. When I was going through my rebellious phase and about three weeks after my 15th birthday, Lizzie popped in to see my mother on the way to a pub. All three of us were in the front room in front of the television. As usual Lizzie ignored me, and indeed I her, and started a conversation with my mother.

After about fifteen minutes she said, "It's his birthday soon, isn't it?"

As if I was deaf or stupid. Though I suspect that I did not simply register in her scheme of things.

My mother replied, "It was three weeks ago, Liz."

My aunt then fumbled in her bag and withdrew a packet of ten Weights cigarettes and threw them to my mother.

"Give him these then!" said Lizzie.

Obediently, my mother then passed the packet to me and said, "Thank your Auntie Liz for the birthday present!"

I had watched each step of this performance, annoyed more with my mother than Lizzie. I threw the pack back to Lizzie and said, "Stick them up your arse!"

At this point Vesuvius erupted. Lizzie stormed out and my mother screamed at me for being rude to her sister, and for showing her up, which was really the greater charge. In retrospect it would have been smarter to have smiled and said thank you. I should not have reacted. Unfortunately, I never learnt from this experience, and there would be many times in later life when I would give into such temptation when I felt insulted.

Although she occupied the position of disapproving witch, like Margaret Hamilton in *The Wizard of Oz*, but without the warmth, Lizzie was essentially a sad figure, living in her own world. Lizzie like her sons had made a bad marriage. Her husband Joe was a heavy drinker and neglected her. In drinking he was very spiteful and took pleasure in winding her up. Each Saturday afternoon, after shopping in Portobello Market, my mother and I would pop into their house for a cup of tea. When 'Sports Report' came on the wireless Joe would awaken from his afternoon nap to check his football pools, refreshed after his lunch time drinking session, and would then spend his time goading Lizzie or contradicting whatever she said. Her response always was to say, 'Oh, shut up, Joe!' and carry on with whatever she was doing. In my memory he was always seated while she was standing over the sink or table doing some domestic activity, making tea, washing up. He the active aggressor and she the passive victim. Despite its persistence and nastiness, she tried to pass off his behaviour as inconsequential banter, which for the audience was clearly untrue. One trick of his goading style was that of latching onto a word and using it in every sentence.

One of his favourites was 'disputing', as in, 'I am not disputing that!'

He would use this three-syllable word as evidence of his cleverness and would savour as well as slur it on each occasion. As I grew older, he would look for occasions to goad me in a similar fashion. In retaliation I would use a word that he was unlikely to know but would certainly struggle with. I can remember offering him the word preposterous' knowing full well that trouble would ensue.

"It's prep… presp… usos… rous… is it?"

At which point Joe obviously forgot what he was talking about and stopped the conversation. It was a cheap triumph, but it provided temporary relief. However, it was this kind of behaviour which supported their view that I should be yanked out of school and despatched to the army where I would learn the kind of discipline that had so richly informed their lives. I would endure these episodes until the time I was ten and able to avoid the shopping trips to Portobello Market.

These absurd episodes would be punctuated by some spiteful behaviour, particularly from Lizzie.

During one very cold winter she was showing off a new pair of boots to my mother when she suddenly said, "These are too small for me. I have had to buy another pair. Would you like them? I will sell them to you for £5.00."

At that time, my mother had more chance of buying a yacht than coming up with £5.00 for a pair of boots, as Lizzie knew well. Even Joe was disgusted by his wife's behaviour.

He picked them up, threw them at my mother, and said, "Have the bloody things."

This was done as much to punish Lizzie as it was an act of generosity to my mother. My mother left the boots, and this proved to be the start of another of their frequent estrangements.

Joe and Lizzie really lived separate lives. Each year she would go on holiday to Dymchurch, Kent with her friends from the Rugby Boys Club. Joe always refused to go. They would visit the pub together each Friday night, but I suspect that they sat apart for a good deal of the evening. In the years after his death Lizzie would talk about her wonderful husband, and cling to her own memories as to a lifeboat. Joe was not wonderful, just sad. The only good thing about their relationship was by being together they ensured that four people were not unhappy.

One thing that did unite them was their dislike and hostility to me. My mother miraculously bought me a brand-new Raleigh bike one Christmas when I was about ten and it was a joy. Every spare moment would find me riding out with friends or on my own. One Saturday I met a friend in the Golborne Road, and I sat astride my bike to have a conversation with him. Suddenly I was grabbed by the arm and Lizzie and Joe demanded where I had stolen the bike from. Despite my protestations they refused to believe me. As a crowd gathered around us, I pushed my bike through them and rode away. When my mother told them the truth there was no apology. However, as on many other occasions she never confronted them about their cruelty.

Albert, or 'Albie', was a very unhappy uncle. He lived with Ivy and her husband Bill in Shepherds Bush for about 20 years after the war. His misfortune started when Grandfather threw him out of the house, although I suspect that it probably started earlier. Why he was evicted I have no idea. During the Second World War he was taken prisoner by the Italians, was then sent to Germany and took part in a death march as the war closed. How he survived it is difficult to tell. When I knew him, he was painfully thin and extraordinarily nervous. For many years he could not walk down the street without compulsively glancing over his shoulder to check who was following. He avoided conflict wherever possible and developed this as a survival skill when living with Ivy and Bill for whom conflict was eternal. Albie and I were to share a bedroom for about two years. The fact that my only memory of that time was his preparations for going out each evening. I was always asleep when he returned.

The key to Ivy, I suspect, was the port wine stain on her cheek, and it haunted her like a curse. It was never mentioned by anyone by her. According to my mum she was the only one who had the courage to stand up to Granddad. But to me she was riddled with insecurity and self-loathing. During the War, as a teenager and young woman she offended her elder sister by chasing service men, and this was also one of the battle areas with her father. Just after the war she married Bill, a discharged service man, and seemed to immediately regret doing so. My mother told me that before introducing Bill to Lizzie and her family Ivy warned them that Bill was fat and bald, had a little squishy nose and that no one was to look at either. Apparently, he was very sensitive about his appearance. At every level this was a stupid mistake on her part.

When Bill turned up wearing his customary trilby Joe and Johnny stared relentlessly at him and one said, “Why has he got a funny nose?”

At which point Ivy ran crying from the room. I never heard what Bill said or did, but I suspect he kept silent. The story, true or not, defined their relationship. The eggshell container of their life fractured under insecurity and what became mutual loathing.

In its own way their marriage proved to be as bad, if not worse, than that of Lizzie and Joe. Ivy tried to numb her pain through alcohol, and as the years passed the level of her consumption began to rise to match her suffering. When I lived with them, I used to help carry the empty bottles of stout and pale ale back to the off license on a daily basis. During this period, I also became a receptacle for all her anxieties.

"Do you think that I am pretty?"

"Am I prettier than your mum?"

"I can cook better than your mum, can't I?"

These questions were often accompanied by tears and periods of silence. These were unanswerable questions for anyone let alone a child.

The important question she never seemed to ask was, "What am I doing in this marriage?"

Although Ivy was financially better off than her sisters it seemed to bring her no happiness. They had television from the time of the coronation onwards; Bill had a van or shooting break. They even had a cocktail cabinet in their front room (We never used the term 'lounge'). These were rare acquisitions for that time and place.

Bill, who had his own problems, found it difficult to deal with Ivy. They would argue, and he would complain about her drinking while she would be abusive to him. Like Albie, I tried to stay on the side lines, but inadvertently ended as a voyeur to another bad marriage. Despite her obvious sufferings I found it difficult to feel sorry for her. She seemed mired in despair and had no energy or interest in doing anything about her problems. She was self-abusive. On public occasions, weddings and funerals, she would become drunk and loud, throwing up her skirts and trying to be provocative. This appeared to be her way of getting back at Bill.

Bill by contrast abused the world, though selectively, for his problems. Like me he had been born illegitimate but was brought up by a woman he called Mother, but who was in fact his grannie. His real mother lived in the same street, but he had been told to call her his sister. It was not until much later that he discovered the real story. Not surprisingly, he never came to terms with this. I do not know what action, if any, he took against his grannie or mother, but he certainly took revenge against the weak. Or that part of the world that would not fight back. For Bill was the classic coward and bully. He could make your life hell if you let him. If you turned against him, he would literally run away, as I was to discover subsequently. Most men treated him with contempt and women with derision. His response was sadism. I can remember him asking my cousin Johnnie to hold a couple of wires from the engine of his car. He then started the motor and laughed as John received an electric shock.

Like Joe, Bill died a good twenty years before his wife, but she never went into denial about her marriage in the way that Lizzie did. He seemed to be forgotten very quickly. She moved in with another drunk and as far as I could tell never mourned her husband. A story my mother told me that when Bill was dying in hospital Ivy refused to see him until someone fetched her. At that point, Albie moved out of the home and probably experienced peace for the first time in his life. He never married. Perhaps he realised that family life could lead to problems.

One early lesson I took from all these experiences was never to stay in a bad relationship. The badness infects not just the principals but all those who come into contact with them and that families have the capabilities to affect the generations unborn.

4
Early Life

Although I knew my mother longer and more closely than any other family member the simple fact is that I never really understood her at all. For most of my childhood and later I felt immense sadness for her because her life was terrible. I can describe what I experienced but with caution. And I soon applied that caution to what she told me about her own life. At a simple level her stories did not make sense to me as a child. I also noticed that she was not very intelligent and had a studious inability to learn from experience. She had no interest in the world about her and tended to believe uncritically stories men told her about themselves. To make matters worse she seemed to have cast herself as a Catherine Cookson heroine struggling against insuperable odds inflicted on her by an uncaring world. What problems came her way were caused by others. She also had an abiding belief that by keeping secrets no one would know the truth.

For example, I discovered that I was illegitimate when I was ten by finding my birth certificate. I had needed this document to attend school camp and my mother had been procrastinating about producing it for inspection. However, I knew where she kept her documents and decided to be helpful. As soon as I read the fact that my birth name was Osborne, and not Clark, I knew what this meant. On being presented with the certificate my mother did say that she had meant to tell me about this one day, but then immediately told me that it was not important, and that I was better off without a father anyway! She illustrated her point by using both Joe and Bill as examples of fathers that I could do without. This was an observation difficult to refute. I did persist for a time in asking questions but would then lose interest with the odd scraps that she would feed me. They were either untrue or contradictory. One of her earliest was that I was a twin, and that my brother had miscarried. When two weeks later I made an appearance, she and the hospital were dumbfounded. Even at the age of eleven or twelve this struck me as an implausible chain of events. I did wonder, based on this, whether I survived an attempted miscarriage. The fact that even now I believe this to be the most likely explanation says a lot about our relationship and our openness.

In 2012 my mother told my wife, Sylvia, the following version of my birth. At the time I was working in another room, and Sylvia came in and related the story. When I confronted my mother about why she had held this back from me, her response was breath-taking. She had never told me because I had never shown any interest in my father!

However, the following is the nearest that I will ever get to an authorised version.

In 1944 my mother joined the Land Army and was based at Bleak House, Catherine Street, St Albans, Hertfordshire (This house is a Grade 2 building now known as Dalton

House). During her service she became engaged to an American paratrooper called Earl Clark, whom she had originally met in London. The seriousness of the relationship meant that Clark spoke to my grandfather about a future marriage. Unfortunately, Clark died during the Normandy landings when she was eighteen. Although distraught, my mother was then comforted by an Englishman, Bill Brinley (or Brindley) whose family owned a guest house in London Colney. The family were originally from Birmingham, but what they were doing so far south I cannot explain. Clark and another American knew Bill, who had been invalided from the British Army after Dunkirk with severe stomach wounds. As a result of this prolonged period of comforting I was born in April 1947 at Brocket Hall Maternity Hospital. Then after the birth moved next door to Lemsford House, which was used to accommodate illegitimate babies with their mothers. I only discovered this when researching for this book. Apparently, I am one of the World-Famous Brockett Babies, which now has its own website and an annual reunion for babies. The institution was set up in 1939, ran for ten years, and managed to produce 9338 babies in that time. None of this was of any interest to my mother. She told me that I had been born in Welwyn, the old town, and, just after our marriage Sylvia and I went on a pointless trip to visit my birthplace.

It is now that we enter Catherine Cookson territory I suspect. My father was studying to become a doctor and though he offered to marry her my mother declined as she did not wish to ruin his career. After my birth his parents allegedly offered to take care of me, but my mother declined this kind offer. Instead, she moved the pair of us, at their request, to the home of Ivy and Bill in St Stephens Road, Shepherds Bush – the address that appears on my birth certificate.

I treat the previous paragraphs with great caution for several reasons. Not least my mother's claim that both Clark and Bill were really kind and good men. This would indeed conflict with her subsequent track record. All the boyfriends that I met were totally unreliable – being a mixture of liars, drunks, unfaithful, rogues, crooks and general ne'er do wells. She used to tell me that all men were weak and unreliable, and given my experience of her lovers I think that that was a fair conclusion. How she expected me to process this observation as a putative man was never considered. But like many of her repeated observations I took them in like undigested food.

In later life several people, including my wife, asked me if I was ever curious about my father and were puzzled when I said, 'No'. I have always taken the pragmatic view that it was pointless to be interested in someone who had no interest in me. When my sister went chasing, and eventually finding, her own father he made it clear to her that his life had moved on so he would be happy for her to leave him alone. All of this caused her great distress, and she laid the blame for his behaviour on my mother. To me it seemed self-evident that he had no interest. Nor did I feel the need to blame anyone but him. A simple difference in our mentalities.

How long we stayed with Bill, and Ivy I cannot say. My

mother said that she returned home one day from work to find our possessions on the doorstep, and she had to walk the streets of Notting Dale to seek accommodation. Apparently, she was also refused admission at Lizzie's home and ended up staying with a friend and her husband somewhere in Ladbroke Grove.

Somehow this odyssey led to a bed-sitting room in Wornington Road, just north of Ladbroke Grove. I only have some vague memories of the time. I can remember being in a cot watching a man and a woman standing at a window as heavy rain ran down the glass. I have no idea of what was happening, merely them being on the other side of the room. I can remember the gas mantles that lit the rooms, ours and the room of an old couple who lived on the same floor. There was a strong smell of toast as the background to these memories. I have no memories of my mother at this time but can remember with affection an older girl who lived in the street shown below who occasionally looked after me.

I was christened on 6 December 1948 at St Charles Hospital, Kensington. The address given on the certificate was 175 Wornington Road, and my mother was using the surname Brinley on the certificate. Sixty years later, when I asked her why I was christened in a hospital she said because the hospital believed that I was going to die.

Not unnaturally, I asked what I was suffering from, and she said, "I don't remember!"

Despite our history together this answer still surprises me. When your mother cannot remember an occasion of your near death it provides some hint of your relative importance in the world.

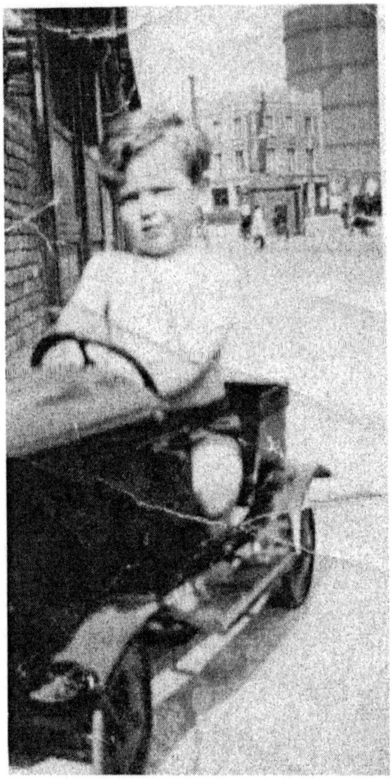

Wornington Road, 1950

Whatever the truth of their relationship, my mother and sister were diagnosed with TB and admitted to separate sanatoriums sometime in 1951. I was processed to go into a children's home for the duration. However, the weekend before we all moved to our respective venues my mother met Ivy in Hammersmith Broadway. Once Ivy was told what was happening, she immediately offered to house me for the duration. Her winning argument being that family must be better than any children's home. My mother found this argument so persuasive that she simply forgot about the nightmare of our previous eviction a few years previously. Nor did she consider the fact that having recently suffered a miscarriage, Ivy's depression may not make her the best of foster mothers. My mother may have also been too distracted by her own illness and worry about the separation from Elaine to give full weigh to her decision making. Whatever, the reasoning process, she had now committed me to two years of hell.

Ivy, Bill and Albie occupied the ground and first floor of a terraced house in Shepherds Bush. The top floor was empty during the time that I lived there. Bill told me that the flat had become empty after the husband had stabbed to death his wife and kids. To add colour to this tale he also said that their ghosts could be heard in the flat on certain days. I was fascinated by a skylight in the ceiling that led to the roof. Bill filled in the gap. He told me that this was the entrance favoured by the murderer on his ghostly visits to the flat. He would announce his arrival by scratching his nails on the landing walls, and, if I listened carefully, I would certainly hear. For Bill this was probably a good joke to tell a four-year-old child.

I shared a bedroom with Albie. He worked on as a labourer, and his weekends were spent at local cinemas, which seemed to be the one interest that kept him sane by keeping him out of the house. We spoke little, as I remember, but used to listen together to an old-fashioned radio in the bedroom. This set listed all the foreign stations like Hilversum and Luxembourg on the radio dials, and their names were illuminated by a backlight. That is all I remember of two years spent with my uncle Albie. I now recognise that the pain that he must have endured during the war had deadened his feelings. It was a house where we were all going to hell in our own ways.

In addition to the maudlin monologues that I heard from Ivy; I was subjected to a constant sniping from Bill about my mother. Not only was she a whore – whatever that was – but she was also receiving treatment in hospital for an illness that she had contracted. What he expected me to make of all these insinuations I had no idea. Later, I would recognise that this was a symptom of Bill's sexual frustration and jealousy, but at the time it meant little to me. We visited my mother once in three years, near the end of her stay, and I could only speak to her through the window. Interestingly, I cannot remember either feeling excited about seeing her or sadness on leaving. On the return journey Bill said that I would soon be able to see my black sister. As I cannot remember having seen a black person at that time or have any idea of what this was supposed to mean, the insult was as meaningless as the accusation that my mother was a whore. My ignorance did not seem to stop Bill enjoying the joke. Although Ivy would tell him to shut up when he made these kinds of statements her heart was not really committed.

Bill tended to specialise in verbal abuse. Although I was smacked as a normal and regular form of punishment, I remember most clearly his acts of mental cruelty. When I was discovered to have been naughty, a regular practice, then I would be locked in the bedroom on the first floor, next to the stairs leading to the top floor flat. Once imprisoned, Bill would scratch on the walls outside and make moaning noises. I knew that he wanted me to cry out, but, because I was not totally sure that it was him outside, I would sit with my back to the locked door and try to pretend that I was somewhere else. It was a strange mixture of courage and fear that helped me get through. What Ivy and Albie thought that he was doing at the time beggars' belief?

Some of the naughtiness for which I was punished included not having a bowel movement straight after a meal. Whether they were concerned about my health or chose to see it as an act of disobedience I have no idea, but it was another regular torment.

One episode that illustrates Bill's sense of humour was that he asked me to 'help' him lay some floor covering in the front room. He laid it from the far wall up to the door. I had been carefully positioned at the far end of the room and he jammed the end of the floor covering against the door, explaining that I was now stuck in the room until he could figure a way out. At which point he went off for a cup of tea. I decided to resolve the problem by cutting my way out of the room using the lino knife. Bill did not approve of my initiative.

This process went on for nearly three years and no one intervened. Albie, I suspect was too scared to create any trouble – he had his own problems. Ivy also had her own torments to deal with. I suspect that Bill was so cunning that most of these events were not even noticed by them or anyone else. Where my grandad was is also a mystery, although his relationship to the three of them may offer an explanation.

At some stage during this nightmare, I can remember standing outside the bedroom door on the first-floor landing and saying to myself, "Either these people are crazy or I am. I think it's them."

I believe that this decision preserved not just my sanity but also my life. However, a lot of my memories and feelings were simply locked inside. It certainly did not pay to be sensitive.

One of the joys of living with them was because Bill bullied the other kids in the street, they got their revenge on me when I played out.

Shepherds Bush, 1952

Many years later, in the early 1970s, my mother asked me to visit Bill because he was dying of diabetes and other complaints. I was shocked at the request because I had last seen Bill when I was 15 and I had gone to physically attack him. My cousin John and his wife were staying in the top floor flat – they would later be thrown out by Ivy – and I had rung the doorbell of their flat.

The door was opened by Bill who said, "What do you want?"

When I told him he pointed me to the stairs.

As I started, he shouted at me, "Get up those f______ stairs, you bastard, before I give you one!"

My reaction was volcanic; I screamed and started to run down the stairs prepared to beat him silly. Ivy and Albie ran into the passageway while he edged into the dining room behind them. I was so frustrated that I started punching the walls. By this time John had descended from the top floor and pulled me away to his flat.

All this was known to my mother, so her request to visit a dying Bill was totally unexpected. At first, I refused to go. However, she persisted.

"He has particularly asked to see you."

That night I talked it over with Sylvia, and only on the basis that she came as well did I agree. When we got to the house Ivy and my mother showed us into the lounge where many years before I had cut the lino. A severely emaciated Bill was sitting in an armchair, and he greeted us with a huge smile of delight. I found it difficult to say much, but Bill was more than eager to explain to my wife the fun that we had experienced together, and what a terrible scamp I had been, citing his version of the floor covering escapade as an example. His obvious delight in explaining all this to Sylvia was astonishing. Although I did not laugh as expected at his stories, I was able to wish him well. That was the last time that I saw him. I still cannot understand what went on in that room with all of us colluding with Bill's pleasure. Nor can I understand why he wanted to see me or why I went.

I have no doubt that my mother inadvertently had gifted him the opportunity all those years ago to work off his anger and resentment against his own awful childhood. He seemed to have no conception that I might have viewed the experience differently. That inability to empathise with other people's feelings seemed such a characteristic of all my family. On the last occasion I saw John at my mother's bedside we spoke about the fight on the stairs. John's dispassionate comment was, 'Bill was a strange man'. As a piece of understatement, it was on a par with saying 'Bobby Moore used to play football'.

One peculiarity about the Osborne family is that having been all born in Hunt Street, Notting Dale, not one of them moved beyond two miles from this address. Lizzie reached the age of 90, my mother 86, and Ivy and Albie both died in their eighties still within the area. Although my mother often talked about moving away, the reality was that she was most uncomfortable outside this place of home. I suspect that the same was true of the others.

The second peculiarity is that throughout their long lives Lizzie, Ivy and my mother were engaged in endless rows and fights with each other. Often the conflict would break two against one, but sometimes it was just one on one. All the fights were bitter and entrenched, and each built on previous encounters. One of the classics followed a 15-page letter sent by Ivy to my mother. This letter was carefully kept under the bread bin for several years and was regularly consulted whenever hostilities resumed, or when she wanted 'to nurse her wrath to keep it warm'.

When I once asked my mother about this endless warfare and why she simply did not just break off the relationship altogether, she looked at me as if I was mad and said, “But we are sisters!”

5
Notting Dale

The Osborne family moved into the area of Notting Dale before the First World War, and most would stay and die there. The area had a majority lower working-class population and a character which shaped me and everyone who lived there. To survive there meant acquiring basic street skills in dealing with a wide variety of characters.

Notting Dale is an enclave situated to the west of the much better-known and better-off district of Notting Hill Gate. As locals describe the place as Notting Hill rather than Notting Dale the confusion is easy to understand. But to clarify the geography, the eastern boundary is Chepstow Road, the northern is the Harrow Road, the southern is Holland Park Avenue, and to the west the area fades imperceptibly into Shepherds Bush. In the nineteenth century Dickens used the term 'Avernus' to describe the area and the human misery contained therein (The Avernus is a crater near Cumae in Italy, believed to be the entrance to the Underworld).

The term used by Dickens was still an appropriate one for the late '50s and early '60s. However, the construction of the West Way flyover in the middle '60s led to a major depopulation of the area which involved families being efficiently decanted to some of the new towns north of London. It was an odd experience to watch people I grew up with disappearing on an almost daily basis for a period of about five years. It was as though my childhood left me before I grew out of it. The subsequent development of the area seems to have simply dropped more people into more flats, so that the population and their problems have both grown exponentially. As far as I can tell, it is still the Avernus.

In the early 1950s the area comprised many very large families, some with up to 20 children. Petty crime and gang life were a major feature of life and recruitment to the ranks started at a very early age. Although it never had the cachet of the East End crime world, Notting Dale was a tough place to negotiate, and, for a boy without a father, a great deal of character to avoid the temptations.

One of my first memories of living in Lancaster Road was sitting on a garden wall in the Spring of 1953 watching the police dig up the garden of 10 Rillington Place opposite. This insignificant cul-de-sac gained notoriety when it was discovered that John Reginald Christie had littered the house and garden with dead bodies. Local people expressed amazement that this equally insignificant man was obviously capable of mass murder. But the general seediness of the man, and his crimes, was typical of the area.

In the mid-1950s large numbers of West Indians started moving in, and Notting Dale started to change quite dramatically in character. At first there was a novelty that some of us welcomed. One of my earliest friends was Winston who used to come to our flat and watch wrestling on Saturday afternoon television. I can remember being both intrigued and jealous of his hair which was always so neat and tidy whereas mine had the look of an unmade bed. In return, Winston would take me to some of the West Indian record shops in the basement flats of Ladbroke Grove. These places were lively, noisy, and very colourful. Neither of those attributes endeared themselves to the locals. Gradually conflicts between white and black youths became fights and then major riots in August 1958. The locus of the local trouble was a house in Bramley Road which was about 100 yards from our flat. For days gangs of youths waited on the streets looking to attack any black people in the area. The ostensible reason for their behaviour was that a white woman had been attacked by a black man. This was probably an urban myth which went unquestioned. Whatever the real reason, the balcony of our first floor flat provided a grandstand seat to watch the fights taking place. Although the police were present, they seemed to be observers rather than officials of the law. At best they could be described as impartial, but the suspicion was that they were on the white side of the argument. One night my mother left me standing on the balcony and ran out into the warring street. She then returned with a very frightened black mother with her son and daughter. All three had been separated from the husband during the fighting. My mother had seen what was going on and had decided to take a policing role. I remain very proud of my mother for taking such a risk at such a dangerous time. She would often demonstrate bravery of this nature and was not afraid to confront men and threaten violence. What was truly odd about this episode is that she remained a racist.

The riots, which were occurring in other places, like Nottingham and Shepherds Bush, ended abruptly when heavy sentences were passed on some of the white youths involved.

However, never one to miss an opportunity, Oswald Mosley started canvassing for the seat of North Kensington in the 1959 General Election. It was a cynical attempt to cash in on the race issue and received an appropriate reward. Having heard about Mosley and his intervention in the East End before the War I was very curious to see both the man and the kind of reception that he would receive. I attended one of his speaking events in Talbot Grove and was really delighted when the very people Mosley believed to be his natural supporters abused his speech and tried to push him and his thugs off their van. At the poll he received a derisory vote of about 8%. He then disappeared to France, never once returning to his 'people'.

The behaviour of the police in the area was always highly questionable. The general perception, which I shared, was that their agenda had little to do with law and order. They could make their presence felt when necessary, and they lacked subtlety. For example, there was a small gang of young men who made a practice of smashing up pubs just before closing time. Like the police, the gang lacked subtlety. It did not require a great deal of intelligence to anticipate their movements and stake out a suspected target pub. Once the offenders came in, the police closed all the doors, and escorted the regulars and staff off the premises. The offenders were subsequently carried out in ambulances. Nostalgic idiots often look on these kinds of episodes as the good old days when the police contained crime.

It was a very tough area, and I suppose it received the kind of policing that it deserved. As a law-abiding member of the community, however, I felt more unsafe with the police than I did with the local villains. Provided you avoided the known areas at night and kept out of gang friendships it was possible to be relatively safe. With the police, however, life was more uncertain. I lost count of the number of times that I was stopped by police and routinely questioned and searched. The only provocation for these activities is that I was on my own, in the early evening or later at night, and returning to Notting Dale, usually from the Holland Park Road. After each fruitless intervention, the police would simply tell me to go home. I never once received either an apology or even a word of friendliness.

All the local villains would complain of being fitted up for both crimes that they did commit and those that they did not. Whatever the truth, the police were never trusted by the general population. Local people tended to sort out their own problems. The police were always the last resort.

Typical of this kind of local retribution was the murderous shooting of Billie Smith by the Bell family and George Baker in May 1960. This arose from a minor dispute in the Latimer Arms public house which escalated to grievous bodily harm, and finally to an early morning shooting. This was an episode that everyone knew about from the start. The only surprise was the relatively minor sentences received – the longest term of imprisonment was 13 years for Ernie Bell – at a time when execution was still the expected sentence for murder. My cousin John was a friend of the Bells, and I can remember one New Year's evening when he brought a group of them to our flat for turkey sandwiches and tea. My mother felt honoured by the fact that they treated her with courtesy. She was of that generation and group that believed local criminals were like Robin Hood, punished the bad but looked after the good. In the same way, she also believed that the Kray brothers had a bad press. One of the convincing reasons being that the twins loved their mother. How this kind of sentimental nonsense arises is difficult to say, but like weeds in a flower bed once it took hold it was impossible to remove. As someone who shared their streets, I took a more pragmatic view of these thugs, and avoided them wherever possible.

Theses thugs did tend to come from the large families, and it was difficult to avoid them because their ages spanned the generations. The only family I became involved, and that was inadvertent, with was the Pugh's.

The bulk of the family lived two streets away and contained somewhere between ten to twelve children – I never did find out the exact number. The one who came looking for me was Charlie, who was about five years older. I have no idea why he was interested in me except I did discover that his 'best' friend, Stefan, had recently disappeared from the scene, and Charlie needed a replacement. Charlie was small and scrawny for his age but looked on himself as a hard man. Hence his desire to have younger friends who would not challenge him. He appointed himself my mentor when I was about 11 years old, largely I suspect because I was so different in outlook and behaviour. Like many people in the area, he was both suspicious and respectful of education. It was certainly not a thing that he wanted for himself, but he liked to be around it so that he could demonstrate his own superiority to those who had it.

His driving belief in life was the need to avoid being 'snide', a term usually applied to counterfeit monies and goods, but which for Charlie described certain kinds of people. He never defined what being 'snide' involved, but I suspect it covered any perceived disloyalty to Charlie. I spent about two years trying to get away from him and his world. What I discovered during this time is how pointless and boring life could be when you get up each day and did the same things.

The family lived in a terraced house in Cornwall Gardens, but all seemed to live in one basement room which was kept in a permanent state of semi-darkness. This contributed to my difficulty in being sure of the number of children. Charlie's mum presided over this room, and indeed the whole house. She was a large imposing woman that it was clearly unwise to cross. A black and white television was on all the time and placed in a high position so everyone could watch. Family members would all eat in this room, wherever they sat, or would bring in cold-water bowls in which to wash their feet or hair without interrupting their enjoyment of the small screen. One of Charlie's family roles was as a 'gofer'. Mum would scream 'Charlie' with a force that could tear bed sheets from top to bottom, and he would be sent to the local grocers to buy doughnuts or down to the fish and chip shop for huge portions of chips. On return these would be dished out to those in the shadows. Cutlery and plates were an optional extra.

Charlie was also a 'gofer' for others, including a local homosexual who kept open house for his friends. He provided a similar service for a brothel two doors away. For them he would run errands and receive cups of tea and menthol cigarettes in return. During school holidays I would go with Charlie to these haunts not believing for one moment that they represented any form of danger. Certainly, if they did it would have been foolish of me to imagine that Charlie would be a protector. Although Charlie saw himself as a hard man, he was just a bully who specialised in the weak and the vulnerable. He assumed that I was afraid of him, but although I was puny and demonstrably not hard, it would have been an embarrassing contest if it had arisen. I did intervene verbally a couple of times when he proposed beating up some unfortunate for simply being scared. For such interventions I faced the accusation of being snide. As the demands of the Harrow Club and school grew then I simply had less time to spend with him. But these kinds of families made me think that I had a kind of privileged life. Whatever I was experiencing was never as bad as the Pugh family life.

Over the years I have listened to others reminisce about their working-class childhoods but unlike them I never found any romance in the situation. If I had been left to survive in this environment without supports, there is a fair chance that I would have become a delinquent of some description. With my family life as well, the combination would have been too toxic to survive. In a way, I did become a delinquent. My rebellion against Charlie and his way of living was almost a rehearsal for the wider rebellion to come.

For already I was learning that it was difficult to break established family patterns of behaviour. Charlie and his family showed me how boredom created trouble, crime produced crime, dependency slowly killed choice, and misery was contagious. For as long as I could remember I found myself on the outside looking in, trying to keep my distance. I knew what I did not want, but no idea what I did want, or even knew what other choices were.

6
Moreland House

My mother was released from the sanatorium in the spring of 1953, and we moved into a council flat in Moreland House, Lancaster Road, right in the heart of Notting Dale. This placed us about half a mile from Lizzie and her family, and about one-and one-half miles from *Ivy et al*. At the time communities were preparing for the Coronation, and I was scheduled to return to Shepherds Bush to take part in their pageant. I still have a picture of me dressed up as a page, carrying a cushion which had held the crown of our Queen. I am singing lustily, oblivious to all, including the tune.

More importantly, at the age of six years I started school for the first time. For whatever reason, Ivy and Bill kept me out of formal education. St Clements Infant School was attached to the church in which my granddad married, and at that time operated a religious regime which included attending a church service each Tuesday morning (I can remember that we also had to attend a funeral service for one of the teachers – a quite daunting experience for six- to seven-year-old). But it was the weekly church services that was really my undoing at the school. Every time that we entered the entrance to the dark church I would pass out and would then awake to find myself in the staff room of the school. After a few weeks someone astutely decided that there must be some problem, so I was referred to a school psychology practice in Pembridge Villas. I attended there for several weeks and was encouraged to play in a variety of ways – dressing up in costumes, using a sand tray, telling stories which were designed to unlock the issues causing the blackouts. My strongest memory was becoming really frightened at some stage and running down a passage where I smacked headfirst into a wall and broke my nose. Interestingly, neither the psychologists nor my mother took any action about this mishap. This resulted in both a crooked nose and a lifetime of sinusitis problems, an unfortunate consequence of receiving therapeutic help. Their final diagnosis, according to my mother was 'Whoever has been looking after this child should not be trusted with a dog!' I suspect that their words were perhaps different, but this version is the one my mother repeated with relish for the rest of her life. She never sympathised with me over this experience, in fact she never asked me what happened or how I kept alive. What she took from the diagnosis was a consoling belief that she was a better mother than her sister. Over the years she would repeat the diagnosis like a mantra.

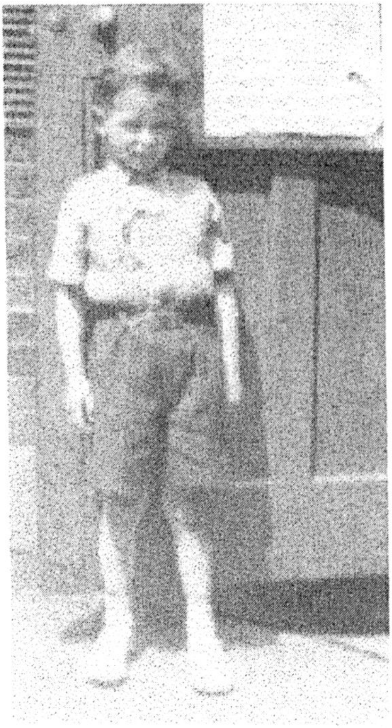

St Clement School, 1953

Although I stopped going to the practice after a few weeks, I remained prone to nightmares and a lifetime of insomnia. For several years, the nightmares were so bad that I needed a night light. The recurring dream involved trying to avoid a witch who had the power to kill by just looking at me.

Many years later I tried to describe the experience, almost as a form of exorcism.

Dream House

Opening the door, he finds
The past already waiting for him,
With trophies of childhood
Hanging on the wall.
Grim heads in shadow
Turning their faces
To the open doorway.

In this corridor he finds
The hunchback cripple
Scuttling through doors
Opening on this corridor
In which he finds
The hunchback cripple
Running away from himself.

The chandelier blooms above the ballroom
While violins whisper in empty cupboards
And soft-spoken words come floating up the stairs,
Meaningless phrases that hang in the air.
And the sound of someone crying.
While the butler with a face like a frying-pan
Unhurriedly climbs the carpeted stairs.

The diagnosis, however, did not stop my mother and me going on holiday with Bill and Ivy that summer. For years I simply accepted that this happened without thinking about what was involved. It was only later, when I was a parent, that I became amazed at my mother's decision. I am clear that if anyone had treated any of my children with verbal or physical cruelty then there would have been a dramatic reckoning.

Many years later my mother trotted out the psychologists' statement about Bill and Ivy not being fit to look after a dog. Her tone of voice was both scornful and judgmental.

I then said to her quite calmly, "You know, I never understood why you went on holiday with them that summer?"

She was silent for a couple of moments and then offered a simple response.

"Who knows why one does these things?"

I let the comment die on the air because I knew that self-analysis was not her strong point and that all I could do was unload my bad feelings on a woman who would have no understanding. A pointless activity for both of us.

Elaine remained in her sanatorium for another six months or so. By this time one of the nurses had become a surrogate mother, and Elaine found it difficult to let go of her. The three of us then came together. Having never really been a family the three years of separation had shredded what little bonding had taken place. We were now essentially three strangers trying to live together. For the next four years Elaine and I had a kind of brother and sister relationship which was largely based on my taking care of her when Mother was at work. By the time I was eleven, and she had started school, we began a long slow process of drifting apart. This was largely a result of the different pathways available to boys and girls in the 1950s – separate schools, separate play but also because it was quite clear that we were becoming very different people.

From the age of seven upwards I started to take on responsibility for doing things while my mother worked cleaning houses to earn some money. All these houses were in Holland Park and Kensington, often owned by elderly rich women. One I particularly remember lived in Camden Hill Square. For some reason she took a shine to me and invited me into her home (I would normally play in the street outside while my mum cleaned). She had a three-storied house with a basement and a chauffeur driven limousine. I can remember climbing the stairs to the first floor, going past a dramatic oil painting on the stair well, and into a kitchen full of exotic smells. She also took me out in her car to visit Portobello Market where she drove beside the stalls, occasionally stopping and ordering her chauffeur to buy fruit. I sat next to this *grande dame* awed into silence. My mum later told me that she offered to adopt me, promising that I would have the best education and upbringing that money could buy. My mum turned down the offer. How she expected me to respond to this situation was hard to say but I never thanked her for the refusal. But this was the beginning of the period when I became her sounding board and advisor. Now I think it is sad that she had no one else to talk to. Whether because of her own prohibition about telling other people about her business or not I could not say. However, when she argued with one of her sisters, and when she started her relationships with men, I would be the audience for all her troubles. She would always ask for advice but never listen to what was said, she would simply repeat the same thing always ending in the question 'Why does she/he behave like that to me?' I realised that these conversations were pointless, nothing ever changed. I was no more than a bass note to her melody.

By contrast, Elaine deliberately kept distance from her, preferring to spend time with our cousin Linda and her mother, Lizzie. Whereas I tried to be a peacemaker to a very volatile and punishing mother, Elaine began to answer her back and be openly defiant. This pattern really became entrenched during adolescence. My mother would return from early morning cleaning to find Elaine still in bed or sloping around the house in her pyjamas. She would shout and scream, threaten to leave or commit suicide. All to no avail; Elaine was unmoved. My only escape from this warfare was to keep out of the house as much as possible. Elaine's indifference was admirable as a defence, but it meant that more grief was coming my way.

As she grew older Mother's tempers grew worse. The slightest thing could tip her off – not answering immediately when spoken to; not washing up a cup properly; any example of Elaine's defiance – and the punishing process would begin. The first stage was a statement like 'That's it! I work myself to the bone for you, ungrateful kids, and what do I get? Nothing? I've ruined my life for you. I am going to put you in a home / kill myself / run off with X___.' She would then go and sit in a separate room in stony silence. After some time, usually hours, she would start some activity, for example, making a cup of tea, preparing dinner, ironing, but without speaking to either of us. She could maintain this period of silence for hours or even days. During this period of moratorium no one could speak, watch television, go out, or read. This was the time for us to suffer.

If these rules were broken there would be another episode of screaming and shouting, and the process would start again from scratch. If I went to apologise for whatever caused the event or tried to speak about anything, she would lift her head in the air and say, 'I don't want to speak to you!'

During these periods of punishments Elaine would take no notice and go and lie down on the bed, seemingly unconcerned. For my mother I was the easy one to manage and manipulate, Elaine remained a challenge that she never ever broke. I have since speculated about the result if I had responded like Elaine, and, my best guess is that Mother would have become violent. There were occasions when I defied her. On one occasion she threw a knife at me. Luckily, it was the handle and not the blade that hit my chest.

On rare occasions we were afforded some respite from this continuing drama. Both my mother and sister were outpatients at the Newton Road Chest Clinic for several years. One of the benefits of weekly attendance was that the almoner arranged for us to have a free seaside holiday for about four years. The first holiday was in a rather dreary Portsmouth; the next two holidays were at Broadstairs; and the final one was at Clacton-on-Sea. Irrespective of the merits of each resort, they each ensured that my mother had to be on her best behaviour; she simply would not allow other adults to see the punishing side we knew so well. Her public reputation was a major deterrent to her anger. So, during these holidays Elaine and I got close to a normal childhood. My fondest memories were of Broadstairs which seemed to be the place for family life and enjoyment. So powerful was the memory that when I retired this seemed to be one place where I could enjoy the peace that I hoped retirement would bring. It has proved to be a particularly good choice.

Broadstairs, 1955

After the trauma of St Clement, I then moved to a junior school. My time at Oxford Gardens School began to open an alternative world. Having missed so much school it took some time for me to catch up. The school contained two kinds of pupils; the working-class boys who came from Notting Dale to the south, and the sons of middle-class families who lived on the northern side, towards Wormwood Scrubs. Because of my friendships I was able to visit the homes of some of these boys and was astounded by what I found. It was my first glimpse of a different, and better way of life.

I remember going to the home of two brothers who had their own playroom with a floor landscaped on a white sheet which included a railway track and a fort. The fact that their mother sat down with us for tea and asked about our experiences at school that day was in some way more memorable than the toys. There was a sense of calm and peace about their house that was intoxicating. The atmosphere was like the seaside boarding houses that I found so comforting.

However, my best friend was Terry Cavanagh who lived in the same road as Charlie Pugh. Terry and I shared a love of sports, and over the years we played in both school and Boys Club teams. Terry was a talented goalkeeper and wicket keeper, but my only talent was for bowling. We benefitted from enthusiastic teachers like Mr Lusby, both head teacher and sports master at Oxford Gardens. Cricket practice for me consisted of bowling over after over at a wicket on a metal plate which sprang back upwards when struck by the ball. The discipline of pitching on a length – designated by a metal plate on the concrete floor – and trying to dislodge a three-penny piece from the off stump had remarkable results on technique. Whenever I resumed cricket over the years, which I did on two different occasions, I was able to produce this stock ball at will. The drawback, however, is that I never received any batting practice with the obvious result that I rarely troubled the scorer. At the age of 38 I scored an impressive 42 not out, supporting a proper batsman who scored 152 not out, and I keep the cutting from the local paper. Sports, particularly team sports, were my alternative to family life.

School was also the place that my love of music began. On my first day there while, waiting to be introduced to my class teacher, I heard a choir sing *The Ash Grove* and *The Lass of Richmond Hill* and I was entranced. My great desire was to join the school choir, but I was always one of the boys that received the customary tap on the shoulder at auditions and was asked to sit down. I did join the recorder group, trained by Mr Barratt, and our speciality piece was *The Dam Busters March*. In secondary school I graduated to playing the cornet, but, despite my love of music, I have proved to be singularly untalented as a performer. But this was another area of my delinquency. Although my family could understand the sports thing, listening and playing music were incomprehensible activities.

It soon became apparent that writing was my skill. As preparation for the 11-Plus Examination we were set many essay topics, the best of which as judged by Mr Lusby, were written out neatly into a special hard cover book which was produced for inspection on Parents Evening. In writing an essay about my family I described my aunt Ivy as a dipsomaniac, a word I subsequently had to explain to my mother. Although she laughed when informed I received a lecture about telling people our family business. I am not sure that she shared this story with Ivy.

In our last year at the school, we had the good fortune to receive lessons from a specialist teacher that the London County Council offered to schools at that time. Mrs Waterhouse, an elderly lady who looked as if she had just risen from her bed after a night of heavy drinking, would read to us for one morning each week. She read *Tom Sawyer, Mark Twain* and *The Thirty-Nine Steps*. She kept a class of nearly 40 pupils spellbound. With great prescience she forecast that whatever else, we would always remember her sessions. She was a great lady who gave a great deal of pleasure to a lot of children. I am not sure whether schools now value simple story telling. If not, it is an incredible loss.

I was quite confident about the dreaded 11-Plus Examination and was almost devastated when I failed. The prospect of attending a secondary modern school which specialised in handicrafts like wood and metal work was a dreadful prospect. However, this was 1958 and the London County Council introduced comprehensive education that year. In our area there was the new purpose-built Holland Park School, which had its own swimming pool, and would eventually attract the children of Labour ministers. The other choice, Isaac Newton was formed from two existing schools about one mile apart. I was given a place at Isaac Newton. At the time I did not know how fortunate this would prove to be.

However, I was already becoming aware that a formal education was a clear line of demarcation between who my family wanted me to be and who I hoped to become.

7
Secondary School

Isaac Newton as a school was still being assembled when we joined in September of 1958. There were two main buildings about ½ mile apart, but we still had to go to a third location for our metal work classes. We started with a school uniform, but we had to wait for one of the art teachers to design a badge in the second term. With great imagination the design was based on an apple tree. Like all comprehensives the classes were streamed; the top level was 'R'; the next level 'M'; and the lowest 'P'. My class was 1R1 which stood for the top class in year 1. After each annual examination pupils could be moved up and down classes and stream. Movement did occur, but the chance for a 'P' student to progress to 'R' was limited. The teachers were a real mix; some came from the old central school and found themselves here when the music stopped on re-organisation. But some bright young teachers had been especially recruited by a committed headmaster. There was a sense of optimism about the school and about our future which was apparent from the first day.

Despite this optimism I was still depressed about my failure at '11-Plus'. Many of my friends from Oxford

Gardens had gone to grammar schools with recognisable names and school badges of which I was jealous. They were also being introduced to the mysteries of Latin. The nearest I would ever come to this world was listening to radio programmes based on public schools. Despite my reservations I started to enjoy Isaac Newton, including learning French and joining the school brass band. At the end of the first year, I came top in my class, which also meant top of the year which included about 200 boys. This came as a great surprise to me. My mother did enjoy the kudos of having raised such a clever son. She used this fact to annoy her sisters, and in the process did me no favours. She was never able to think things through. My success to them was an obvious example of why education was such a waste of time. Instead, I should have been out earning money, paying my mother back for her sacrifices.

At the end of the second year, I repeated the feat of coming top. Under normal circumstances I should have been eligible for a transfer to a grammar school but the headmaster, Edward Davies, a man to whom I would become extremely grateful, refused the opportunity on my behalf. Not unnaturally, he wanted his school to build a reputation and if people like me left then there would be little chance. I was told this some years later by a teacher, Brian Benjamin, who would have a great influence on me and other pupils in my year.

However, my achievement was not maintained. I began a terrible decline that mystified my teachers and my classmates. The truth was that my mother's behaviour became crazier and more punishing, and I was finding it difficult to cope. As I entered my teens, my mother's turbulent love life went into overdrive. Whether it was a reaction to bringing us up or she heard a clock ticking, I do not know, but she began to try and make up for lost opportunities. Like other families we were reliant on the tallymen. To be a successful 'tallyman' you required two key skills; an ability to charm the women into purchasing from you; and an ability to judge when a particular woman was near the limit with her debts. At that point you only turned up each week for the money, and the word went out to other tallymen. The flats in Moreland House were good territory, and my mother was an easy target for the over-friendly salesmen with a quick line in chat. One of the earliest of her boyfriends, almost a warmup for the real thing, was Wally.

I came home from school one day to find my mother mooning over a calendar which showed a moated house. When I asked why she was so curious she told me that Wally's family lived there. At the age of 11 or so I tried to persuade her that this was unlikely. Jewish tallymen did not live-in listed buildings, and, if they did, they would probably have chosen another profession. My impeccable logic fell on deaf ears. Where men were concerned my mother knew best.

For whatever reason, certainly not because of my arguments, Wally was quickly replaced by what would prove to be the love of her life. Jock was a large tough man from the Gorbals with blonde wavy hair. He charmed all the housewives, but, unfortunately for them, my mother went out and caught him. Little did she realise that single women held a particular attraction for tallymen. Once 'caught' his charm began to fade very quickly. He took her out for a drink in the early days of their courtship, but then became an occasional late-night visitor for bed and breakfast. It was clear to me what he wanted, and it was not a long-term relationship. I still do not know whether he was married or not. For my mother this was the real thing, the love of her life, a view that persisted despite the late-night visits and early morning exits. On these occasions he was often drunk and clearly had just arrived for the sex or a bed for the night. Sometimes he would knock on the door. More often, he would climb through the bathroom window. This was meant to be a discreet form of entrance. His visits meant that at midnight or later, Elaine would be ejected from the bed that she shared with my mother and forced into my single bed. This was not something that she looked forward to and something that I hated. Amazingly, my mother believed that neighbours were unaware of the situation, which betrayed a remarkable capacity for self-deception.

The relationship staggered on for about five years, and was marked by arguments, long absences and recriminations. During the absences, my mother used to spend hours speculating about his movements. She once sent me on my bike to contact him at an address in Holland Park. Where she got the address from, and why she did not go, remain mysteries. When I reported back that he was not known at that address she accused me of going to the wrong place. So, his absence was now my fault. On another occasion the three of us were off on a journey and on route to the bus stop she spied Jock in a pub. She rushed in and started an argument with him while Elaine and I stood outside waiting on the pavement. All the pain and sorrow that she accumulated would be turned on us. Sometimes she would accuse the pair of us of being the main obstacles to her prospective life with Jock. If we were not there, then she could be happy. In addition to her resentment was now added the threat that she would up and leave us at any time. The idea that Jock would disappear into the sunset with my mother was ludicrous. His idea of paradise was a pub. My mother did not see this or want to see this. She tried to make him jealous. She then had short-term sexual relationships with similar kinds of men – tallymen, layabouts, bingo callers and crooks. When these men stayed the night, we awaited the inevitable fistfight between them and Jock. It never happened. But I came close to having that experience.

During one of these warring periods my mother confided in me how miserable she was and how Jock was ruining her life (If we were not ruining it then someone else certainly was). She insisted that she had to get rid of him but did not know how. I, fed up with the litany, said not to worry, the next time he turned up I would tell him to leave. I was about 14 years old, weighed about 8 stone, and was not an impressive build. Jock was a 6ft drunkard and notorious street fighter who, as far as I know was never bested. So, for weeks I went to bed each night waiting for the coming confrontation. This period of waiting was not helpful for my insomnia. He eventually turned up at 1:30 in the morning and I answered the loud knock on the front door. Calmly I opened the door and managed to get my rehearsed speech out. 'My mother does not want to see you, so go away!' There was a long silence. Then two things happened; one, the puzzlement on Jock's face slowly began to be replaced by anger (Thinking was not his speciality, and drink did not help the process).

At the same time, my mother ran from her bedroom pushed past me and said, “Go to bed, and mind your own business.”

Whatever relief I felt at the rescue from violence was completely lost in being made to look stupid. Although she later explained that her intervention was for my benefit, I felt used and betrayed. Her life was a drama, and I could not find the exit, hence the decline in my schoolwork.

The climax to this relationship occurred in 1962. I returned from school one evening to find my mother with her head in the gas oven and the gas on. In retrospect, I realise that her timing was careful. When I dragged her out, she started screaming and crying out that she wanted to die. I eventually got her into a chair and calmed her down. She then explained that she was six months pregnant. Not only did she not want another child, but she could not stand the shame of her pregnancy. I suspected that she had also found out that Jock had no intention of being a father to the child. I persuaded her that a visit to our GP was a better option. This doctor was well known for being patient friendly and had a pattern of supplying my mother with antibiotics and other drugs almost on request. A drug habit that she would maintain throughout the rest of her life. Unsurprisingly, my mother was admitted to the hospital for a ‘procedure’. As far as I know. I am still the only person she spoke to then or since about the pregnancy. I still not sure whether my sister, who was 12 at the time, knew about this. My mother believed that the secret was safe with us.

The public story was that she was going into hospital for a minor procedure, a ‘scrape’, dilation and curettage. Elaine went to stay with Lizzie, and my cousin John came to look after me. Ironically, it was at this time that John started his relationship with the woman he would eventually marry, and probably got her pregnant in our flat.

Whatever the 'procedure', a baby was born alive, was christened John Michael, and then died in the delivery room. A few days after her release from hospital my mother took me to Kensal Green cemetery to visit the grave of my half-brother. Until then I had not even thought about what had taken place, for me the whole thing had simply been another problem which had to be managed. When we arrived, the hole was covered by loose planks, and we were able to see a small white box lying sideways against an adult coffin in a pauper's grave. It looked as if the box had been chucked down the hole and the gravedigger could not be bothered to jump in and straighten the coffin. As I looked at this mess below the enormity of what had taken place hit me, I felt both sick and tearful. This was a dead baby; no one knew or cared about his existence.

My mother said, "Don't you dare show me up! Stop that and come with me!" (A ghostly echo of what her father told her at school) At which point she went off to confront the gravedigger. She was able to deal with her anger with him. As for any other feelings I have no idea how she managed. We never ever spoke about John Michael again. Not that day, not that week, never. Until I told my wife many years later no one else knew about this little secret.

I could discern no effect on my mother. She continued the awful relationship with Jock. But something inside of me had crumbled. There was a dead child and I had been complicit in his death. No one knew about him but me. No one cared for him but me, and my care was not worth a light in the darkness. I could not grieve; I did not know how. I could not speak to anyone about this. My anger and resentment grew but I did not know what to do. The one prohibition my mother repeated endlessly was, 'Don't tell other people your business.' I became angry and rebellious, not at my mother, but at life in general. I stopped wearing school uniform, got into fights, started bullying boys in my school. Although I lived in a violent area, I had developed the survival skills necessary to avoid most trouble because I had no interest in fighting. I had learnt who I needed to make eye contact with to avoid fights. I also knew whose eye contact to avoid achieving the same end. I had learnt how to react when meeting gang members on the street, and I had learnt how to appear tough, and walk away. These lessons were mostly effective in that I only fought when presented with no reasonable alternative. Mostly I could talk or bluff my way out of trouble. Now I started to look for trouble and started acting stroppy. On one occasion the gym teacher caught me wrestling a boy to the ground in the classroom. He instructed us to have a boxing match in the ring. David Biggs, the boy I bullied, with his superior height, reach and strength knocked me all around the ring. The humiliation was far worse than the physical punishment. My anger grew. I then punched an inoffensive classmate, Norman, in the eye, for reasons I cannot even remember. I split his eye lid and he was taken to hospital. The next day his mother came to school and asked to see me personally. The teacher asked me if I would be willing to speak to her. Out of sheer bravado I said yes. She did not rant and rave, but calmly explained how I had hurt her son Norman both physically and emotionally, and the effect that this had on her and her husband. This was a woman who loved and cared for her son and was brave enough to front up the lout that had caused him pain. I looked at her with my stupid thug face and did not have the grace or the compassion to apologise. But every one of her words dripped like sulphuric acid on my skin. For the first time in my life, I felt shame and though I walked away from the experience that feeling has stayed with me always. It is an episode that still haunts me.

All this rebellion came to a head when I confronted a sadistic maths teacher. I threw a punch at him in the classroom. Luckily, it fell short. But such behaviour was standard grounds for expulsion in any school. The headmaster, Mr Davies, aware of my growing pattern of misbehaviour, obviously realised that something must be wrong at my home. He stipulated that I make a public apology to the teacher, which I hated. On this condition I could stay on at school. My classmates, who knew how much I hated the teacher, just treated me as a big-mouthed coward, which was a fair assessment. Just to keep going I closed internally. I did my lessons, played sport, and kept myself to myself. Having crossed that line of decency I could no longer see myself as being different from Bill, Jock, Ivy, Lizzie and my mother. I was one of the Osbornes carrying on the family business of stupidity.

After the abortion my mother's relationship with Jock began to deteriorate, and he was succeeded by a line of similar ne'er do wells. All of whom treated my mother with little respect. They would come and go when they wanted. Our flat was used to store stolen goods on a couple of occasions. She even took part in the robbery of a boutique where she worked. She allowed her boyfriend to tie her up while he robbed the shop. She was eventually untied by the police and told them her prepared story. By living at home, I also became complicit in all these activities; nothing was kept from me. Apart from having to put up with the behaviour of her boyfriends, I know became fearful of her going to prison and us being put in a home.

The amazing thing to me was that everyone seemed to think that she was a model mother and told her so. Living in a small block of flats comprising 20 families and a common courtyard it is inconceivable to me that our neighbours were not aware of what was happening. We were certainly aware of what they were up to. Gossip was like the measles, quickly shared. However, my mother seemed to operate on the principle that if she did not believe it to be so then it did not happen. She certainly had a reputation for violent aggression locally, which might explain why nothing was ever said to her face. On several occasions she confronted men and women and saw them off. However, I could never understand the perception of many of her friends who would tell her what a wonderful mother she was.

I became sick of hearing them say to her, "You are a good mother to them, Alice."

Then they would turn to me and say, "I hope that you know how lucky you are?"

This public image was so important, and she truly believed that she was a good mother sacrificing herself for her children. The sad thing was that at some level I believed it. She had looked after us, gone through hell and taken us with her. Without her what would the world have been like? This conditioning was relentless and effective. How dare I complain? All my anger, sadness, and fear were buried beneath a patina of gratitude.

As for me, I scraped a few ‘O’ levels and was due to leave school at sixteen. We had all attended a meeting with a careers advisor whose sole suggestion was to join the Civil Service. He tried to sell me the benefits of working for HM Customs and Excise. I am still not sure who experienced greater boredom during the meeting – the advisor or myself. Fortunately, my headmaster intervened again and promised to see if he could arrange a grant that would enable me to stay on to study ‘A’ levels. I was desperate to avoid the Civil Service, so I had an anxious wait at the end of the summer term in 1963. My mother did not object to the extra two years if the grant came through. During my school career the only interest my mother showed was in attending prize days. Not surprisingly, her sisters were less than impressed by this turn of events. Everything I now did justified their awful warnings. I was the burden pulling them all down. I remained the pariah of the family.

8
Harrow Boys Club

At the age of 11 I made the wisest decision of my young life; I joined the Harrow Boys Club. This was one of many such institutions set up by public schools in the late-Victorian era to help the poor. At the time I looked on it merely as a place of safety, but it was so much more. I met the man there that not only kept me out of goal but who was to become the nearest I ever had to someone who cared for me.

The building still stands, but now functions as a community centre offering a range of valuable services to a still-impoverished community. The centre has received large sums from charitable bodies that have provided it with a range of extensive facilities and refurbishing. Back in the 1950s the entrances were on the other side of the building, that which now faces the elevated motorway that stretches from Shepherds Bush to the Marylebone Road. The construction of this fly-over in the 1960s was to have a devastating effect on the immediate community. It was to sever the link between the Club and my generation.

The main entrance to the Club led up a short flight of stairs from the street level. The door opened onto a hallway at the end of which was the manager's office. The desk inside was lost under a sea of papers. The office belonged to Lewis Ashman or 'Lew' as he was commonly called. On the left-hand side of the hallway was a door into the main hall. This housed a full-size snooker table, and then three table tennis tables of variable quality. The best was always at the far-end of the hall and was therefore the property of the better players. Just beyond this table, at the end farthest from the door, was a stage on which stood a small snooker table and two dartboards. On a busy night movement on the stage could become extremely complicated for everyone, unless carefully choreographed.

At the front edge of the stage was one of the key features of Club life; the Dansette record player. This was in use most nights, and my memory insists that it was the same small collection of LPs that were always played during eight years. This was Lou's music, and shaped the taste for good or ill, of my generation at the club. The collection included *Oklahoma!* and *Oliver*, but the overwhelming favourite was the stage version of *West Side Story.* Night after night, year after year, I absorbed the same melodies. It shaped the repertoire of songs sung in the Club van on our ways to matches or holidays. Even now, when I hear the opening notes of the *Prologue*, I am immediately pitched back to the age of 14; table tennis bat in hand, dancing around the floor developing my backhand drive.

There was a small mezzanine floor above the hall and Lew's office. The room situated here was only ever used for the construction of kayak canoes. Canoeing was a strong feature of Club life, and some of the keener members would pay for, and build, their own canoes, often as part of their quest for a Duke of Edinburgh award. Although I became addicted to canoeing in my later years at the Club, I only visited this room about three times in eight years. I had no desire to master the skills required to build a canoe.

The second entrance from the street led down to the basement. The external door led straight into our 'sports hall', in which we practised five-a-side football. The hall was tiny and made worse by having a low ceiling supported by metal girders and a set of wall-bars down one of the long walls. The skills required to simply run and turn without dashing your brains against the fixtures and fittings was demanding enough. To have to also practise passing, shooting and tackling, required acute survival skills. When we had to practise heading skills a ball was suspended from one of the metal girders of the roof, and the height was varied by the trainer, tugging on the rope, every time we jumped. As this took place no more than four feet away from the back wall it was a miracle that we all managed to avoid being embedded in the masonry.

The very sight of this facility would have bought a health and safety inspector out in a cold sweat, and the club would have been condemned on the spot. But for us it had the allure of Wembley.

Just off the hall was a small room with three showers. My memories of this room are anchored by a discarded jock strap. I would swear that it remained on a wall hook, unclaimed, for the whole eight years of my membership. In some way it symbolised, for me at least, a memorial to the unknown sportsman.

On the other side of the hall was a coffee bar, which housed the television. This was only ever used for watching mid-week football matches, or, events of great importance, like the General Election of 1964 or the assassination of President Kennedy. Generally, the club was for doing things rather than watching others do them.

This room connected with the table tennis room above by a long dark staircase, which had the effect of muffling sound. Lew would occupy this room later in the evening. When the Club opened on a Friday his place would be by the large snooker table on the first floor. He would stand next to the 'Forthcoming Events' board, welcoming each member as they arrived, collecting weekly subscriptions, and seeking to enrol members into some representative activity for the Club. 'Ah, Dear Boy,' he would say. 'We are trying to get up a cross-country team for Saturday. Can I put your name down?' He always called me 'Sunshine'. I was probably the least sunny adolescent in West London, but I would always smile in response. Only Lew would call me that in tones of affection rather than irony.

The building was merely a shell; for Lew was the Harrow Boys Club. He was the force of nature that gave it life, shape and value. He devoted most of his waking hours to the Club and the boys, and we knew what it cost him. His commitment to us was never discussed or acknowledged publicly, but we returned it with a respect that was no less binding. When he asked you if you were free this weekend for a canoe race, you said, 'Yes,' and thought about it after. It was only usually on the Saturday that I started to question what I had let myself in for. We volunteered because Lew asked us, and because we were a team.

Taking part in a canoe race from Hampton Court to Tower Bridge on a freezing wet Sunday in December requires commitment. Trying to light and smoke a Players

Weight cigarette while paddling the canoe demands a level of personal creativity that only the desperate can manage. When I was eventually hauled out of the canoe by the river police suffering what felt like hypothermia, I saw this as my problem. None of the other boys or Lew had to be rescued. I just felt sorry that I had let the team down. It was simply another example that would have sent a safety officer into a state of apoplexy.

When I first met Lew, he was about 36 years old. He was around five feet ten inches tall, well built, with dark curly hair that was always immaculately groomed. Periodically he would grow a full-set beard, reduce it then to a moustache, or return to being clean-shaven. These changes were as frequent as his attempts to give up smoking. Lew was a heavy smoker who despised the habit. He therefore gave himself the worst of both worlds. He also gave us hell about our smoking, particularly when he was smoking himself. He would use his own addiction as a moral example of why we should not smoke. He would stop us smoking until we reached the magic age of fifteen. But he never stopped nagging us about the habit whatever our age. This was the only kind of censure that he offered.

He was very handsome in a square-jawed English hero fashion. In certain lights he looked like Ronald Coleman, other times like Errol Flynn. What really distinguished him in our company was his accent and language. He sounded and spoke like David Niven. He would address me as 'Dear Boy', as a variant of 'Sunshine'. Many years later I shared my observations with him about his handsome appearance and he modestly brushed them off. After a brief pause, he then said, 'When I was younger some people did think that I resembled Laurence Olivier.' This example of vanity dressed up as modesty was pure Lew.

I, like the other boys, simply accepted this old-world charm because it was Lew. Other adults would not have dreamed of speaking in this way to us. Nor would we have accepted such liberties. But we accepted Lew for who he was. It was the least we could do. Such acceptance was a rare experience for most of us. Like most adolescents we lacked tolerance for others who happened to be different.

It was also clear to me at an early age that Lou was gay. Whether he practised or not I did not know and could not care less. I suspect that most other boys had a similar belief. The amazing thing was that in the homophobic climate of a 1950s' Boys Club it was never mentioned. Being adolescent boys, we were deeply accusative of anyone who was in any way effeminate or narcissistic. Being called a 'poof' was the deepest insult that could be offered to each other. In his own way, Lew helped me, and I suspect others, to value people for who they were and what they did rather than for their colour, sexual orientation, or religion. His toleration was remarkable. As a born-again atheist at the age of 17 I spent two hours arguing with Lew about Christianity. He listened, accepted, and then offered his own views. Not once did I even suspect being patronised.

He was prone to hysterical reactions though. When disappointed by others he could sulk. And if he felt slighted, he would seek revenge. For example, once at the annual camp on the Isle of Wight, six or seven of us pinned him to the ground and splashed some cold water in his face as a joke. He avoided the perpetrators for the rest of the day. The next morning, he awoke each of us in turn with a wet sponge in the face. Having evened the score, he could then return to normal.

Similarly, one year on a holiday in Sitges, Spain, I, and another boy, managed to lose the teapot while we were doing the washing up. The loss was not discovered until next evening at a campsite some miles away. On this occasion he treated the pair of us like criminals for two days, taking every opportunity to complain about his loss. Given Lou's need for tea this was a serious privation. The amount of mileage that he had driven from North Kensington to Sitges gave him every reason to complain.

Near the end of his life, I asked him where his commitment came from. He said that his values derived from his experiences in the Air Force, and that his aim was to help each boy achieve his full potential whether it was physical, mental, or spiritual.

It is now impossible for me to think about Lew without also thinking about music. Not only did he love songs, but he had a beautiful voice and took great delight in sharing his gift with us.

His voice had the pitch and timbre of Gordon McRae or Howard Keel. He would sing all the time. But for me, best of all, were journeys in the van. Then we would hear his repertoire. *The Surrey with the Fringe on Top, Maria, Tonight,* and *The Foggy, Foggy Dew* among others. Every time he would start to sing the boys would ritually groan 'Oh, turn it in, Lew!' But, within minutes the protests would stop and some of the braver – more musical – boys would join in with the song. As I got older and more confident, I would ask him to sing two of my favourites, *O What a Beautiful Morning,* or, *The Soliloquy from 'Carousel'.* To listen to those tunes being sung by a man was to receive a precious gift. The gift was not just the song but also his delight.

He is the only person I have ever met who could take such obvious delight in all around him. The object may have been a song, or sunlight on the river, but what he felt he wanted you to share the experience. Not only did his face shine with joy, but he would invite you in with his characteristic. 'My, stars and garters, look at that!'

One of his declared aims was to bring the worlds of Harrow School and Harrow Boys Club together. Each year members from the school would attend summer camp on the Isle of Wight. At the two camps I attended there was no problem with the integration. Within a couple of days new social groupings quickly formed which crossed the boundaries of School and Club. It was clear that both sides both enjoyed and learned from this experience. One school member I remember with great fondness was David Wilkinson. He became a guitarist with the 'Band of Angels', who would later include Mike D'Abo as their vocalist.

In return a selected few would attend various activities at the school or use their facilities. During the summer, small groups of us would go up in the evening and use their swimming pool 'The Ducker'. This had a curved kidney-shape that had the deep-end in the middle. It also had changing rooms like bike sheds, open to all the elements, and passing passengers on the local bus could watch us as we undressed.

I was also fortunate enough to play a cricket match at the school. My memory of the match was over-awed by the pavilion in which we took tea. Even the watercress in the sandwiches seemed doused in history. I look on that day as my Rupert Brooke period.

I was also invited, with Lew, to attend a performance of *The Tempest* by the Old Harrovians in their Elizabethan-style theatre. I even visited the tomb on which Byron supposedly lay when composing his poems. I was able to experience a different world because of Lew.

During my period of rebellion, I even stopped going to the Club. Because of my implicit vow of confidentiality, I would not tell even Lew what was happening. I simply drifted away. By the time I started my 'A' levels I was back full-time at the Club, and my relationship with Lew became closer. We would spend time going to concerts at the Albert Hall, sharing books and records. He became the friend that I needed to see me into the world of the arts. He allowed me to be normal.

When I left school and started work our contact ended. I was too old for the Club and was developing other relationships, not least with the woman, Sylvia, who would become my wife.

In 1969 I was married and living at Southfields, near Wimbledon. One morning on my way to work I got onto a tube train and saw Lew in the carriage. I rushed over to speak to him, but he was obviously dreadfully embarrassed, and did not want to speak to me. He had left the Club and looked unshaven and quite shabby. He did not want to talk to me and appeared to be embarrassed or ashamed. I wrote down my address and asked him to contact me, but I could see that he was too uncomfortable and would not take up the invitation. With a mixture of respect and grief, on my part, we went our separate ways. He would later tell me that at the time he was working a night shift as a telephonist.

It would be 30 years before I saw Lew again. A local historian was commissioned to put together an exhibition to re-launch the Club after a major development programme was funded by the Prince's Trust. She contacted me and I offered pictures as well as stories about Lew and the Club. Near the end of our meeting, she said that she was visiting Lew the following week to collect his memories. Astonished, I asked her to ask Lew whether he would be happy to see me. The reason for this formality is that I knew that Lew was extraordinarily private, and I was very conscious of our last meeting. However, my concern proved ill-judged, and we agreed to meet at his flat in Windsor. I was delighted beyond belief. For years I had bored Sylvia and the children with my stories of Lew, and now I was going to meet him again. On the journey over from Horsham, where we then lived, my delight was beginning to fracture into fear. Would it/he/I be, OK? Can you pick up after all that time?

Within 15 minutes of meeting all the years dropped away and we could have been bridging a gap of two weeks. Lew was now living in a one-bedroom flat and at the age of 79 was suffering major health problems. Having lived always such an active life being housebound was a great trial. Luckily, I was now able to return a fraction of the favours that I had received. I would drive him out to his favourite places along the River Thames, and he could recount stories of those outings with Club boys. He came to my house for dinner and met the family. And I am especially grateful that for the last three years of his life he spent

Christmas Day with my family. Sylvia and the children fell under his spell, and he became fascinated by their lives and interests. Near the end of his life, I wanted to tell him how important he was to me. I deliberated about doing so many times but was fearful that I would get it wrong and inadvertently upset him.

I drove to his flat one afternoon and said that I was just coming for a social visit. However, I wanted to thank him for being the father that I never had. I was extremely nervous about saying this and started to explain that many of the Club boys, including me, had lived difficult lives as children and how particularly important the Club and he was to us during this time. I started to explain that I had no idea who my father was, and that this did not matter because of my relationship with him. At this point he stopped me and just said 'Dear Boy' and I saw tears in his eyes. Out of respect for his feelings I did not continue the conversation. The fact that I never had the guts to tell him that I loved him still haunts me. I console myself with the thought that he understood what I was going to say. But I am not sure. Unfortunately, he was the kind of Englishman who kept his feelings locked away.

His health continued to decline. He was already suffering from deep veined thrombosis, then suffered a heart attack. He continued but suffered major intestine problems which led to having his bowel removed. When I visited him after this surgery he simply said, 'Now I want to die.' All I could say was, 'I understand.' He accomplished his mission within three weeks.

Along with other representatives from his life I was asked to speak about Lew's funeral. Each of us was limited to a maximum of three minutes. This is my speech.

I want to tell you about a gifted man called Lew Ashman. I met him at the Harrow Boys Club in 1958 when I was 11. 44 years later I am still a member of that Club.

Lou was very handsome, with dark curly hair and a beard. Recently I told Lew that he used to look like Errol Flynn and speak like David Niven. He dismissed the comparison, but then told me that it used to be said by others that he looked like Laurence Olivier. Only Lew could combine modesty and vanity in the same sentence.

Lew made absolutely no concession to the difference in class and background between himself and most of us. He had the gift of treating with respect a group of teenagers who believed that they were out to change the world. Of course, he changed our worlds.

In addition to the vast range of sporting activities, Lew made possible so many new experiences. In my case, this included many first visits.

- *To a West End theatre*
- *To the Proms*
- *Covent Garden*
- *Abroad*

Perhaps Lew's greatest gift was that of sharing his delight and wonder in all around him. He found delight in everything.

- *Sunlight on the river*
- *A glass of wine*
- *Tiramasu or ginger ice cream*

He would stop suddenly, his face alight, a smile of pleasure on his lips, and then invite you with 'My, stars and garters, did you ever see, taste, hear?'

And you stopped what you were doing to enjoy not just the experience but Lew's delight in the experience.

He disappeared from my life for 30 years... 1969–1999

Then through a third party we met once more, and he took me to his favourite pizza restaurant in Windsor, and it was the Lew of old.

He met my family and they all fell under his charm.

For, as we know, music has charm. When driving the Club van to events Lew used to sing. And I particularly enjoyed, 'O, what a beautiful morning.' And it always was a beautiful morning, even when it was raining, even when it was afternoon, because we were with Lew.

And we used to sing a Club song back to him.

I would like you to imagine a van full of boys, in muddy football kits, returning from a match, and singing:

'We are the 'Arrer boys.
'We know our manners.
'We fight with spanners.
'We are respected.
'Wherever we go.
'Doors and winders open wide.
'Ever seen a monkey eat brown bread?
'Ever seen Lew-Lew's curly head?
'We are the 'Arrer Boys.'

We sang it with love and respect. Thank you, Lew, from us all.

There were a couple of other boys from the Club at the event. Afterwards they told me that I had spoken for them. They gave me great pleasure.

9
Club Life

However, it was during these years at the Club that I experienced, if not a substitute family life, then a collegiate life that was both pleasurable and therapeutic.

I played football and cricket for Club teams from 1958 to 1965. In the case of cricket, I had some talent to justify my selection, but for football it could only have been a mixture of my obvious enthusiasm, and charity on the captain's part, that carried me through the years.

As a footballer I lacked basic skills, fitness and any sense of positional play. But this was not the problem it might appear. Luckily, this was the era when a coach's sole contribution to developing skills was to ensure that everyone was physically ill during pre-season training. This was one area where I could offer a contribution as great as my colleagues. That task completed, the coach's contribution was limited to standing on the touchline urging all and sundry 'To get stuck in'. The only personal tuition I received was instructions such as 'To do your best'. This was often said plaintively rather than with any great conviction.

This was the era of the 5–3–2 formation and was played with all the fluidity of quick-drying cement. Our football boots would have been rejected by a miner as too tough to wear, and we kicked leather balls that assumed the specific gravity of lead every time there was a touch of dampness in the air. It was bad enough to kick, but we were also expected to head the thing on a regular basis. Therefore, the one skill that most of us did develop was the ability to just avoid making contact with our heads. We had to be really good at that to convince the coach.

A boy's position in this formation was determined by factors such as physical size, lack of mobility, levels of aggression and stupidity. Skills were only a consideration for the two or three members of the team who would automatically play wing half or inside forward, the interesting positions. The rest of us were sorted as follows. The tall muscular boys whose lack of mobility was more than compensated for by their sadism became fullbacks. The tallest boy in the team would play centre-half, while the next tallest played centre forward. Small speedy boys would play on the wing and attempt to avoid psychotic full backs. Any boy with a high pain threshold would be a 'natural' goalkeeper. All other considerations for selection were secondary. Tactical discussions never advanced beyond the need to score goals at one end while defending against them at the other. Some teams did require further information about which end needed to be defended or attacked.

For reasons that were never explained to me I was selected as a left-winger. The obvious facts that I was right-footed and could not run at speed or at length were never seen as obstacles. My only qualification for the position was a political one and bouncing off full backs helped me understand the true meaning of the phrase, 'lumpen proletariat'.

Each player had a choreographed routine for matches. Full backs patrolled their respective grooves from goal line to halfway, being encouraged to kill anything encountered on route. The wingers operated the same grooves in the other half of the field; their task to avoid fullbacks. Centre forwards patrolled the line from centre circle to, and often through, the goalkeeper. Only the inside-forwards were allowed any form of lateral movement. But no one was ever allowed to pass the ball backwards. Any deviation from the above rules created absolute confusion, especially for the coaches.

The only way we departed from this pattern was the selection of our goalkeeper. Terry Cavanagh was an inspired choice in the minors, he possessed some skills for the job. Unfortunately, as we grew older and taller Terry did not keep pace. Some aberrant Welsh gene meant that Terry did not really grow. This failure did not inhibit his love for the position, and it would have taken a captain with a heart of stone not to select him. His bravery was formidable; he would leap for crosses into a group of players and then disappear. When the referee blew his whistle Terry would be found in a heap on the floor clutching the ball securely to his chest, stud marks tattooed on his jersey. He would also dive with monotonous regularity at the feet of centre forwards and be knocked senseless as they kicked for goal. We developed a theory about Terry. We believed that he did not have a bone in his body longer than six inches, hence his remarkable ability to avoid fractures.

Our coach, Albert, was an ex-professional of Queens Park Rangers, from whom we received our football shirts. He was a well-mannered gentleman with a rural accent, who was beginning to find changes in society a bit bewildering. He was of that generation that believed the centre parting the height of sophistication. He also had a particular fondness for players like Terry whose ability to take physical punishment was remarkable. Whether similar experiences in his career accounted for his bandy legs was never discovered. However, to see him in a pair of shorts and running towards you was a sight to behold. When he tackled it seemed as if you had been surrounded.

We played our home games on our own ground in North Wembley. Team members would meet the Club van at the North Pole Public House and be driven to the match. The journey was accompanied by several significant rituals. The more senior boys would occupy the positions just behind the driver or at the door. The younger, or newer members would sit between these two groups and keep quiet while their elders held forth on issues of the day. The accumulated wisdom contained in our van would not have disgraced an academy. I can still remember the considered view that Muhammad Ali, or Cassius Clay, as he then was, would be systematically dismembered by Sonny Liston in their first big fight. As he was one of my heroes, I took these warnings as dire predictions.

The following week my elders had re-written history. It was evident to all, they maintained, that a boxer would defeat a fighter every time. The Ali victory demonstrated the very point. The fact that I could found both the pre-and post-match comments full of profound insight says something about the awe in which I held my betters.

During my time, particularly in the seniors, I had the fortune to be a member of very good football teams. Over the years I managed to accumulate a nice collection of London Federation of Boys Club medals to prove the fact. On good days, and with a strong wind, I sometimes helped to contribute something positive – like failing to miss heading the ball, or getting the opposing full back booked by the referee for grievous bodily harm of my person. Other times I made up the numbers.

However, in the juniors, for reasons I still do not understand, we experienced one season of abject failure. We were so bad we could not have recorded a score on a dartboard, with a lance. The lowest point that season came in a match against our arch-rivals, the Rugby Club. By halftime we were losing 7–0 and required a miracle. It duly arrived in the shape of our statuesque right-back, Alan Eames, a boy not normally noted for delivering sporting miracles. More by luck than judgement he managed to dispossess their left-winger out near our corner flag, and with the ball at his feet he ran towards the halfway line. By the time he reached his destination at least three members of the opposition had attempted to tackle him without success. Destined for glory he ran on, towards their goal line. We followed in his wake, some of us suffering nose bleeds from being so far up field in this game. He rounded their full back, looked up to see us stretched in a line to his left, and then he fashioned a superb cross that could be tapped into the net by a wooden leg held by an idiot.

It proved to be a moment when time stood still, and the fickle finger of fate decided to tickle our fancy. As the ball crossed our inside right swung and missed. The failure of our centre forward was harder to explain. He missed by a mile. I was now our last hope. I could already see the funny side and was giggling as I also missed the ball. We all watched it roll, inexorably and slowly towards the corner flag. The despairing groan from Alan rolled around the empty spaces of the park as he lay on his back with his hands raised in plaintive plea. The noise was like the woeful whine of a beached whale. It told of a despair that could haunt continents. One of our defenders tried to rescue the situation by shouting, 'Great cross, Alan!'

This proved too much for the rest of the team. Despite all the natural considerations for a teammate the laughter started. Slowly, and politely, at first. Even some of the opposition joined in, while poor Alan wearily trudged back to take up his position, knowing that his day of glory would go unrecorded by a goal.

In after years Alan would recount his version of the event. With each telling the number of tackles he evaded increased, as did the total number of plonkers who had missed the greatest cross ever seen in the history of the Club. In some versions we had more forwards than the whole Football League. 'Alan's Game' would be recalled and described more often than our successful matches. Alan told the best version. But to be fair to him it was always in response to a request from one of the other boys.

In the year that I sat 'A' levels our team was playing as well as I can remember. The start of that season did present us with an experience that puzzled us all. One of the regular players introduced a small Glaswegian into our football training. Despite his lack of size Jock played at centre forward with an energy and tenacity that was quite impressive. Such was his commitment that no one begrudged him his opportunity in the first team when our regular player was out injured. We all admired a trier even though we could not understand a word he said.

When the match kicked off our diminutive Scotsman made a bee line for their centre half and tried to run through him. He bounced off. Every time he got the opportunity Jock repeated the charge. It always led to the same result. It was the nearest our team ever got to a tactical innovation. Their centre half looked bemused, but as it was quite clear that Jock was the only one suffering, he allowed it to continue. Just before half time the referee lost patience and decided to book Jock. Back in the dressing room there was an attempt to talk him out of his strategy but the guttural responses we received were not re-assuring. Within a short time of the re-start Jock went straight back to business and was sent off by the referee. This was one of the few times that a player from our team had been punished in this way. We were mortified. On our journey back to the Club we travelled in silence. His career with the Club was over, and we all knew it.

I never knew where he came from or where he went. The team member who had introduced him never mentioned him again. I can only assume that Jock was like the Wandering Scotsman, companion of the Flying Dutchman, doomed to travel the football clubs of the world to see if he could manage to last a full 90 minutes on a pitch. It would have to be some form of penance for a major sin.

We were to experience another embarrassment during this season that really tried Lew's patience. We were involved in two cup competitions and in an early round of one of them we found ourselves drawn against some very poor opposition on their pitch in North London. The weather had been bad for a couple of weeks and the pitch looked like the Somme battlefield. As we kicked off in heavy drizzle there was an ominous feeling in the air. The old leather ball kept sticking in the mud and all attempts at kicking failed to move it more than a few feet. Although we spent most of the first half in their goal area, we could not get the ball in the net. We hit the bar, goal post, had shots kicked off the line, and missed from point blank range. The harder we tried the more farcical our performance became.

At half time Lew berated us and explained that a replay would have to take place on this dreadful pitch in one week's time. The effect of the talk was to make us even more self-conscious about our failure. The game deteriorated from the re-start. We could not string together two consecutive passes. We fell over, collided with each other, kicked air, sprained muscles, but still could not score the goal required. As the half wore on Lew became incandescent with frustration. His 'Dear Boy' echoed across the ground like rifle fire. At the final whistle Lew gathered us up, marched us to the dressing rooms and told us to collect our clothes, as there was no time to shower. He then drove us back to the Club. We sat in the van covered in mud, shame and remorse, trying desperately hard not to break into hysterical laughter. It was only in the comfort of the showers, out of Lew's hearing, that we called to allow the laughter and tension to emerge. For us to have played any worse would have required detailed coaching.

Growth Experiences

Although football and cricket were the mainsprings of Club life lucky members like me could be talked into what can only be described as growth experiences.

Lew asked me to captain a team in the London Federation of Boys Club Chess Championship one year. Our team of three was keenly awaiting the first match. But when the draw was made, we discovered that our opponents would be a team from Southam Street Youth Club. At this time, the early 1960s, Southam Street was a notorious no-go area for anybody that had a desire to reach adulthood. Seen on a map it would stand next to a dragon. The possibility that there was a chessboard in the area was a major curiosity. That there might be three chess players as well was verging on the miraculous. I queried the match with Lew who assured me that we would be met by the youth leader and introduced to their team. Short of feigning an illness, which I seriously considered, there was no alternative but to play.

As we walked up the Golborne Road that Tuesday evening not one of us believed that this was a good idea. We had all volunteered for unpleasant assignments in the past, but this was beyond our imagining. We debated the possibilities of life and injury, and then agreed that whatever happened we should stay together. This desire was more romantic than practical. Between us we could not produce one serious muscle, and certainly no desire to put it to use. However, as we entered their club to an ominous silence the youth leader introduced himself and explained that the matches would be taking place in separate rooms. At the first door he ushered our number three player in to meet his opponent. At the next door he did the same with our number two player. As I was led in to meet their champion an image of feeding-time at the zoo had already formed in my head. We were being fed to wild animals. As the door opened my heart stopped. Sitting in the other chair was Bluey, a huge West Indian, and the living terror of Isaac Newton Comprehensive School.

Bluey was well known throughout the area, though not for any intellectual prowess. In the three years that we had attended the same school I had never heard Bluey speak. One reason for that is that I had resisted all desire to get close enough to listen. He was well over six feet tall and had muscles in every part of his body. When he frowned, which he seemed to do often, his forehead resembled a ploughed field. Just looking at him from a distance induced waves of cowardice to wash through my body. When he walked across the playground, he left behind a vacuum of boys holding their breath in case they inadvertently offered offence. I had never been so close to him before. As I was introduced to him Bluey looked me straight in the face. I squeaked a timid, 'Hello, Blu…' and stopped awkwardly. I realised that I did not know whether anyone actually called him by that name, or how he reacted when they did. This did not seem to be the right time to discover that I had made a social error.

As I sat down, I realised the strength of my moral dilemma. I guessed that he probably would not be the hardest opponent to beat at chess, but I had no idea about how he would respond to losing. I was dubious about another person being stupid enough to offer him that experience. If they had any sense, they probably offered him the joys of success. On the other hand, could I face my teammates and tell them I had lost at chess to Bluey? They would suspect me of throwing the match. I know that if the positions had been reversed, I would have milked the situation for all it was worth and accused them.

The board had already been set up and Bluey was sitting behind the white pieces. I decided to forego the normal courtesy of competing for the choice of colour. Bluey seemed happy enough with the white players, why should I argue? Bluey moved his first piece, pawn to king four. I concluded that he had obviously mastered some of the basics. For the first few moves my strategy was simply to avoid antagonising my opponent, so I stopped breathing. The silence became oppressive. I could hear the clock ticking and Bluey's muscles creaking as his frown became more intense. I could also feel my lung tissue begin to tear with strain.

I felt reckless enough now to move my knight and call 'Check'. Bluey looked at me and then at the board. I could feel a glacier form along my spine. Bluey moved his king into another line of check. I decided to break the news gently. 'You are still in check.' Bluey pondered this new problem and looked at me once more. I smiled, in what I truly hoped was a sporting fashion. It was difficult to tell how my gesture was being received. He moved his piece out of check and I began to speculate that I might have to be the first person to explain to Bluey the concept of checkmate. I wondered if he might agree with my explanation. I hated the idea of having to describe this, particularly as my tongue seemed to be undergoing some form of paralysis.

As the Ice Age deepened, I began to breathe firmly but not too loudly. It was time to move to an end game.

Within another five minutes Bluey was becoming acquainted with the experience of continuous check. I thought that I detected some small signs of irritation on his part. At one stage he breathed audibly and some of his eye lashes moved. We seemed to be moving to a crisis.

I offered a very tentative 'checkmate'. Bluey shifted in his chair but sat looking at the board. He held this position for an incredibly long time. Whether he was coming to terms with defeat or was considering ways to express his disappointment I had no idea. I could not take my eyes away from the row of knuckles that studded his hands. In the lamplight they glowed like hot rivets.

Slowly he raised his head and looked me directly in the face with the coldest of eyes. He then pushed back his chair and stood up. I suddenly found my little paw in his right hand and my arm was shaken. On reflection, it could have been my whole body. I felt truly moved by the experience. 'Good game,' he said, and then left the room. I staggered into the corridor in search of the youth leader. He told me that my friends had finished earlier, having achieved victories, and that they had decided to return to the Club. I started to babble about the pleasures of the match and how well we had been received. I was also recalling the solemn pledge we had made as a team about staying together until the end.

It took me some time to realise that I could have lost without jeopardising the team score. I could have died in vain.

I focussed all my thoughts on gaining the other side of the railway bridge that led back to comparative safety. As I walked down Southam Street I had an overwhelming desire to run but I resisted the temptation. I was thinking that I had done the man thing that Ernest Hemingway was always wittering on about in his novels. I had faced death, trembled, but survived. I was not now as other men. The bell had tolled for me. Bluey and I had stepped up to the line and faced each other; man against congenital coward. I had passed the test. What could I not do?

But I should have known, Lew had other ideas.

The London Federation of Boys Clubs mounted a public speaking competition and Lew decided that I should form the necessary team of three that included a proposer, the main speaker, and the seconder. The three of us would have to talk for about 45 minutes in total. The speaker would take most of that time, but the other two parties had also to contribute at least five minutes each. I agreed to give it a go if I could pick the subject and we could coerce two other Club members to support me.

When Lou told me he had talked Terry Cavanagh and Alan Bateman into the enterprise I had a wicked idea of a suitable subject. What both Terry and Ray really needed, I decided, was to discuss the relevance of modern poetry as a superior form of psychological insight. It was all the motivation I required to produce at one sitting the three set pieces. I wanted all three of us to die bravely, rather than limp out on the back of a boring topic like 'Ten Funny

Things that Happened to Me', 'My Favourite Holiday', or 'Playing the Game'.

As it transpired my forecast of the topics picked by other teams was not too wide of the mark. By contrast ours would be a jewel in the making. Terry would acknowledge in his proposal that I was going to pour scorn on C.P. Snow's thesis of the two cultures. Alan would then insist, in closing, that the 'The Waste Land' by T.S. Eliot told us more about alienation than any current sociological thesis. I could already hear the sharp intake of breath that would accompany each syllable we offered.

I knew that both Terry and Alan would enjoy standing up and saying these things – eventually.

I gave each of them a copy of the text, and Lew arranged a rehearsal at the Club, so that we could confirm the timings of the different sections. Luckily, both Terry and Alan decided to go along with the activity as an experience. Terry was even willing to adopt my suggestion of looking dismissive as he mentioned the name of C.P. Snow. His sneer was something to behold. The fact that our presentation was as lamentable as both the subject and the text that I had produced, added a certain distinction to the proceedings as far as I was concerned. I honestly felt that we would offer some novelty value in the competition. We would be the 'Rolling Stones' of public presentations dirty, dangerous and unpredictable.

I was as surprised as anyone when we won the first round. This probably said far more about the poverty of the competition than any excellence on our part. Our performance had not been improved by the opportunity to rehearse. It had only helped develop our awareness of how awful we were. We had now added some performance anxiety to the proceedings. I would have settled for some ignorance of this fact.

Our prize was to attend a second round at a school in Willesden a couple of weeks later. We obviously had not thought this through sufficiently. On this occasion, winning equalled further suffering.

This second event involved more groups and the whole atmosphere was far more formal and professional. At the end of the evening each team received feedback in public from the judges. When our turn came, we received compliments on our brave choice of subject, and were also told that the recital of poetry required great skill. The senior judge then went on to say that with practice I might be able to acquire the skill. This comment brought him a round of laughter and me an urgent desire to find another area of potential fulfilment.

What still impresses me about our two performances is that neither Terry nor Alan ever asked me, or anyone else for that matter, any question about a word of the text that they had to read. They were either better read than I gave them credit for, or they had decided to treat my arrogance with the indifference that it merited.

The Isle of Wight

My visit to the summer camp on the Isle of Wight took place in the momentous year of 1962. While the rest of the world was worrying about the Cuban missile crisis, I was preparing for residence at a finishing school. For summer camp was where one learned how to deal with some important life issues, such as how to pull girls. It was a chance to draw on the tribal wisdom possessed by our elders, away from the prying eyes of the adult world.

In many ways Alan Eames had already been one of my mentors for some time. Earlier in the year he had taken me to Burtons in Portobello Market to buy my first suit. The possession of a suit was a basic requirement, according to Alan, for attending camp. As a veteran Alan was able to take me through the process from picking the cloth through to the final fitting. For reasons I never questioned he had insisted to the tailor on a military instep on the cuff of the trouser so that it rode over the break of the shoe. As boots with Cuban heels were very fashionable this appeared to make sense, in theory. But when I saw the trousers at the first fitting, I harboured some treasonable doubts about Alan's concept of fashion. These doubts increased when my family asked me why the front of the trouser was higher than the back, and had the tailor made a mistake? Apparently, this design feature was new to them as well. I retained my faith in the mentoring process despite their scorn.

In general, the cut of the suit would have suited a tall guardsman, but on the slight frames of boys under five feet five inches high it must be confessed, at this late date, that the style verged on the eccentric. Nonetheless, we now owned the most important requirement for a camping holiday – a suit. Only by being a member of the Club was I able to discover this major secret about camping holidays.

When we arrived at the campsite in Sandown during the heat of August our first concern was how to take care of the suits. As we entered our allocated Bell tent Alan Kimber discovered the most obvious place. He undressed, put his suit on a coat hook, and hung the hook on one of the ventilation holes near the top of the pole. Even while he was still looking pleased with himself, we all watched the hook and attached suit slowly slide down the tent as it widened the ventilation hole. The final tear was quite dramatic.

This action helped to decide who slept on which palliasse. For the next two weeks Alan was able to sleep with one eye on the stars and reflect, particularly during rain showers, on the disadvantages of being innovative. Although we all told him how stupid he had been the moment the tear opened, the truth was that each of us would have done the same.

This was my first experience of camping, and the facilities were Spartan. We had two toilet tents, and each contained a chemical lavatory. For washing, we had a large wooden table with metal wash bowls next to a cold-water tap. This stood open to all the elements at the other, and lower, end of the field. Morning ablutions were a trial of endurance. The only times I had heard about people walking through dew-filled fields it was as some romantic act of being in touch with nature. I cannot remember any of us discussing our morning experiences in those kinds of terms. Unromantically, we spent most of the two weeks wearing either shorts or swimming costumes during the day, and no shoes. But the nights were different. We saved ourselves for the nights and dug out our suits.

One of Alan's tenets for a gentleman was that anyone could wear a good suit, but a true mark of distinction was having highly polished shoes. So, each evening, before dinner, we sat in a circle buffing away at the shine on our shoes, discussing the ways of the world. However, to achieve the real accolade, it was necessary, according to Alan, to *polish the instep of the shoes.* The theory behind this practice was that when crossing his legs, the young man would dazzle his beloved with the instep of his shoe and the thoroughness of his approach. She would recognise this as an inalienable sign of class, and the next step that the pair would take would be up the aisle of Westminster Abbey. Although I continued this polishing practice for many years, I cannot remember anyone being impressed. Many were curious. I do remember being asked several times why I adopted the practice.

Most of the advice offered during these seminars concerned how to pull a woman of *class.* According to our elders the female world divided between scrubbers and class acts. Although the former certainly had their uses all serious energy needed to be directed at the latter (Why we referred to girls our own age as women I never fathomed).

How we fitted into this class structure was never discussed. The assumption behind these discussions was that we were desirable objects. Self-awareness was not well developed. We cherished the naïve fantasy that it was the male who exercised choice and controlled the world; women had to wait and discover their fates by being chosen.

For example, another elder told us how to avoid losing control and being snared by some designing woman.

"When you go to a party," he said, "and there is a chance that you might get drunk then you need to take some protection. After a couple of glasses systematically work your way around each woman and propose to them. Then, if you do get drunk and start misbehaving you have already proved that you should not be taken seriously."

We all nodded sagely in response to this, colluding in the belief that we were surrounded by women who were already finding our attractions so hard to resist. The fact that we had a wealth of evidence that most of us could not pull a needle through a sock, let alone pull a girl, did not seem to invalidate our collective view of the world. Some of the more serious among the group probably took notes.

Another piece of advice concerned the following strategy for saving energy and time. On meeting a new woman ask her immediately if she will sleep with you. If she says no, then you have probably saved yourselves hours of frustration. If she says yes, agree the time and place, and then you can settle down for an unhurried drink. At the time, this seemed like the wisdom of the ages, more than making up for every visit to the chemical toilet or the early morning wash. And to think some parents paid for children to attend finishing school we had got such wisdom for free!

During this holiday my hero, Alan, was sorely tested, found wanting, but was able to stage a remarkable recovery. One evening he picked up two attractive girls at a fairground and then invited me to join them to make up the numbers. The evening was already late, and the girls wanted to return to one of their houses so that they could play some records. Alan flirted, negotiated and determined, to his own satisfaction that we were onto a winner. I was less sure. When the two girls conferred their giggling, did not fill me with a hint of future promise. My suspicions were over-ruled by Alan who saw their behaviour as their anticipation of pleasures to come. For his part, Alan attempted to keep them entertained with his range of impressions that stretched from Pat Boone singing *Speedy Gonzales*, to Jimmy Durante and

The Guy That found the Lost Chord. With some reluctance I followed in the wake of the entertainer, eager to learn.

Every now and again I would interrupt the trio to ask the girls how much further we needed to walk. Their assurances satisfied Alan, but I was already calculating the time required to get back to Sandown and meet the van that would return us to the campsite. My calculations suggested problems. I grabbed Alan to share my concerns.

"Don't worry," he said, "we can sort that out in the morning."

As I struggled with the subtext of this response the girls stopped outside a house that had lights in the lower floor windows. One of them said to Alan, "Just wait there, we'll check out that everything is OK." The pair of them disappeared into the house and we stood outside on the pavement. After a few minutes Alan offered the suggestion that they were just playing hard to get. After ten minutes his patience wore thin, and he knocked on the door. It was opened by a rather tall man who asked our business. Without missing a beat Alan responded, 'How far to Sandown?' As the man gathered his thoughts, we both started to back away. I never did hear the answer.

This anti-climax needed to be managed. Alan did not fail me.

"Neil," he said, "I'm losing my touch. I used to be very good at spotting lesbians."

In a summer when people were worrying about nuclear missiles, or mourning the death of Marilyn Monroe, I was attending finishing school and learning about lesbians. As we sat in our in our tent, watching rain drip on a depressed

Alan Kimber, and polishing the insteps of our boots, we were hungry for new experiences.

Each year an American graduate would stay with Lou for the summer and would then attend camp on the Isle of Wight. Most of the ones that I remembered were friendly, energetic, willing to get stuck into most activities, and very respectful. The American this year, Chuck, fitted the general pattern but was feistier than most. One of his ideas, before we got there, was to systematically swim around the Island. Somewhere on the ferry over, he shelved this ambition. Whether it was due to our laughter or his own observations it was difficult to say. However, he proved to be the inspiration for another experience that year.

Our campsite was surrounded by those of other youth organisations, including one for the Boys Brigade. Although we attempted to contact some of the other groups the Boys Brigade was not one of them. They were not a popular body. There were many reasons for their unpopularity but the one that really irked was that they would raise and lower a large Union Jack to open and close the day. Both these activities were accompanied by the sound of bugles, which, we all agreed was not the most musical of instruments, particularly at those times of day, particularly on this Island, particularly in August. But, as our priorities really lay elsewhere, picking up girls for instance, we were happy to live and let blow. Not so Chuck. The ceremony irritated him beyond belief, particularly as the bugles disturbed his morning sleep. He wanted revenge and reasoned that if there were no flag then the bugles would remain silent. It was the kind of wish-fulfilment that only an American could produce.

Accordingly, he formed a commando group of about ten and informed us of his plan. The essentials of the strategy were that while the rest of us created a credible diversion, he, our daring leader, would sneak in during the confusion, lower the flag, and steal away. He had drawn a plan of their campsite, which was situated, on the down slope of a cliff, and the perimeter was protected by a small wood and wire fence.

The only safe line of approach to their camp would be from the shore, up the cliff, and through the far perimeter. On completion of the attack, we would run down the slope, through their camp, and disperse through campsites on the other side. This planned exit would also disguise where we came from, because our camp was at least two fields away. In the noise and confusion, they would have no way of tracking our movements.

They sounded 'Lights Out' at 10:30 p.m. so we had to execute our plan in the hour before, under cover of dusk. By nine o'clock we had taken up our respective positions on the fence. Our plan involved some of the boys running down the hill, kicking over tent pegs, overturning equipment, and generally making a hell of a noise. I was given the job of kicking over one of the strange sentry boxes that dotted their perimeter line. It was only when we got into position that we realised that they were in fact toilets. The attack was due to start dead on 9:30 p.m. to achieve the maximum effect of surprise. We had solemnly synchronised our watches, darkened our faces and hands, as part of our preparation. Having sat through years of war films we all knew how to dress for these occasions.

One obvious weakness in our plan is that 30 minutes is a long time to wait, particularly if you wanted to remain hidden from spying eyes. At 9:25 a man decided he wanted to use the toilet. As he approached the box, I heard him say, 'Is there anyone there?' Believing that I had been seen I decided to try and bluff it out instead of leaving him suspicious. I stood up in silence expecting to be asked for an explanation. Incredibly, he failed to spot me, and having shone his torch in a couple of places, he entered the box. I was now in a torment of anxiety. Could I really push over this box with a man inside it? This was a moral rather than a physical issue. With the guy ropes loosened on the box I just had to push the top slightly and the slope of the land would achieve the rest.

As the minutes crept inexorably to 9:30, I heard the warning shout from my colleagues, closed my eyes, and did my duty. As the box hit the ground I was already up and running. But because of the excitement I was going in the wrong direction. As I scampered to the top of the cliff, I could hear noises and screams from the camp and saw bursts of torchlight strafing the ground. When I got to the cliff top, I dropped down the other side and was away, like a goat on amphetamines. I had no awareness of my feet touching the ground. By all rights I should have fallen and broken every bone in my body. Some survival instinct guided my feet in safety, but in the wrong direction. I got lost.

It was after 10:30 when I got back to the tent of our commander in chief. As I entered, he smiled, and pulled the edge of the flag from under his sleeping bag. We had triumphed, and there had been no casualties, on our side at least, or prisoners taken. I departed to the main tent and enjoyed my cup of cocoa before retiring for the evening.

The following day, the farmer who owned the land visited every campsite with someone senior from the Boys Brigade camp. We escaped detection through the simple expedient of lying. Lew, I'm sure, had his suspicions, but wisely never shared them with us. The American had his trophy and the rest of us felt we had gained some satisfaction from a job well done. The Allies had triumphed again.

Somewhere in America, I am certain, there is an elderly American who still sleeps with the flag under his bed, and, I hope, he occasionally brings it out to embellish the tale he tells of days long gone. Of a time, when silently and efficiently, a troupe of commandos executed his plan of action against an unforgiving enemy.

Our parents had seen off the Axis Powers, we had dealt with the Boys Brigade.

The Seniors

Lew had established a committee of senior boys as part of the structure for managing the Club. This was part of his strategy for developing responsibility. There was of course a management committee to which Lew himself reported, but we were held accountable for most of the activities undertaken by the Club. So, I was given responsibility for water activities – swimming and canoeing. Others had to report on football, cricket or other competitive activities. The duties of a committee member involved attending the activities, organising them, and then reporting on them once a month at committee meetings. In my case, this meant going to the Monday evening sessions at Walmer Road Baths, any swimming galas, and the Sunday morning canoes trips on the Thames. The committee would also make decisions about special events and present an annual report on parent's evening. This was my introduction to the wonderful world of committees.

The reward for this service was to be taken out to dinner at Quaglinos Restaurant and Night Club where the management committee staged the annual charity dinner on behalf of the Club. To attend this event, we were required to wear formal dinner suits that were hired from Moss Brothers. We were also expected to bring partners. I was the only member of the committee still at school, in the first year of 'A' levels, and I did not have a partner. To spare my embarrassment Lew arranged for me to escort a very nice student teacher to the event. I had already met the girl at the Club and a delightful evening seemed to be in prospect.

We had been receiving information and advice about this dinner for some weeks and one thing we had been repeatedly told was not to eat during the day as the meal would be sumptuous. I took this advice literally and had eaten nothing since breakfast. When I returned from school that day, I was more concerned about dressing correctly than I was about my keen appetite. By the time I arrived at the Club to meet the others I could hear my stomach rumble.

It was a tradition to go to the house in Eaton Square of committee member, Laurence Verney, and have some cocktails before dinner. As this was my first experience of drinking cocktails, I decided to enjoy it. At some stage during my second drink, and in mid-conversation, I had this odd premonition that I would pass out cold. My sense of the future was quickly fulfilled. As I slumped to the floor, I had an image of myself, with trousers bouncing up and down at the end of my braces, like a cartoon character falling through the air. When I was brought to, I tried to pass the experience off as an accident. I can remember saying, 'I don't know what came over me.' When I was walked around the square to clear my head, I confidently insisted that all was well. Unfortunately, my confidence was misplaced.

The restaurant at Quaglinos was on the lower ground floor and was approached by an elaborate staircase. Clutching my escort in desperation and attempting to summon every ounce of sophistication that a 17-year-old drunk could muster we descended the stairs.

I am not totally sure on what step it occurred but I somehow managed to catch my foot in the hem of my escort's dress. My entrance to the dance floor was completed by a slightly imperfect swallow dive that brought me up close to the nearest table and the group assembled there. The only saving grace about this was that it diverted attention from my escort who fell to the earth with a bump and proceeded to beat a tattoo with her backside on each of the steps. Somehow, she seemed to preserve some form of dignity. On stopping, she simply rose, without breaking step, and walked to our table.

While the rest of our group went to join her, they seemed to be strangely preoccupied with the seating arrangements and the decor. I eventually staggered across to apologise to my escort only to discover that her sense of humour was truly exhausted. My guess is that even now she would probably find it difficult to discover the funny side of our night out. She had met the escort from Hell. Being totally incapable of reading the ‘go away and die’ look with which she favoured me; I persisted and made the situation worse. I racked my brains to recall any advice of my erstwhile mentors that might help. Even I could appreciate that a proposal of marriage was inappropriate. It was not even a good start. At some stage in the evening, I did attempt to communicate through an intermediary, but this proved equally pointless. The only intermediary she would have entertained on my behalf would have been a medium. I do remember spending a lot of the evening alone at the table trying to hold a conversation with a waitress about the meaning of life. The conversation seemed very one-sided. In fact, I cannot remember the waitress saying much at all. I can also remember a long ride back to the Club that passed in a blur of silence.

My entry into the competitive world of writing started innocuously enough. On arriving at the Club one evening Lew showed me a flyer advertising the dual level entry form for writer of the year. Firstly, you entered a piece of prose or verse, no restriction on numbers submitted by an individual, to the local area competition. In our case this would be the London Federation of Boys Clubs. Secondly, if you managed to win the regional prize then you were automatically entered for the National Association of Boys Clubs Award. After my less than triumphant debut in the world of public speaking, I thought that this time I would avoid prose and try for a poem. This was a courageous decision because, so far, I had never written a poem in my life.

Surprisingly, and with very little effort, I managed to produce on the next day a fragment of Shakespearian blank verse that began as:

I stand, unsure of any strength of choice,
Upon the brink of adult life...

Although I tried a couple of other attempts over the next week I decided to stay with this verse. On the following Friday I gave this entry to Lou. The actual competitions were some months into the future. Although the competition went to the back of my mind, I continued to write verse regularly and found it a great satisfaction. In that sense, I had already won a prize.

Occasionally I would show some of my verses to Lew but, apart from us, no one else knew about this development. Therefore, it was with some surprise that Lew informed me one evening that I had won both competitions. This meant two different prize-giving ceremonies some weeks apart. The first event involved the London Federation of Boys Club, and the prize giver was Viscount Amery. This meant that I had to take the day off school and attend their function somewhere in the city.

The presentation for the NABC award was even more prestigious. For this I had to take another day off school and go to St James Palace to receive the award from the Duke of Gloucester. The prize-winners for a whole range of NABC awards were required to spend the day together, and there were introductory activities and briefings to be completed before our visit to the palace. At the palace itself we were kept in a special room, and when our name was called, we had to enter a large hall filled with a range of dignitaries, as well as an audience of parents and Club officials. Each presentation was photographed, and we later received this as a memento of the event.

All through this process I felt like a pretender because my entry was the first piece of verse that I had ever written, and, as such, could not possibly deserve the award. The quality of my later work was far better. But the obvious delight that the occasion gave to Lew helped assuage my feelings of guilt.

One of the dignitaries at the ceremony was Frankie Vaughan who, as an ex-Boys Club member in Liverpool, devoted a huge amount of his time to the cause of Boys Clubs. One example of this, was that he was headlining at the festival hall that evening in a show called, ‘Clubs are Trumps’, to generate money for the NABC. All the people who were involved in the day’s events received complimentary tickets for the show. Other performers on the bill were Benny Hill, Johnny Dankworth and Cleo Laine, and it proved to be a great evening.

The undoubted high spot of the whole event, however, was one enjoyed by my mother.

As she made her way up the stairs to the festival hall, she was poked in the back by a man who said, “I know you.”

As she turned around, she recognised Frankie Vaughan.

Catching her breath, because she was a great fan of his, she said, “How do you know me?”

He said, “Your son won the Writer of the Year Award. You must feel very proud?”

She was able to dine out on that story for months afterwards.

My reward was being taken to Covent Garden to see a production of 'Tosca' by Lew and another Harrow Club Committee member. I had no idea what to expect and was stunned to find that we were sitting in the front stalls. I am pleased to say that I have retained most of the details of that production.

Winning the award blew my secret as a writer, and I had to go back and face my friends and colleagues at Club and school. Fortunately, there was no adverse reaction, and I was able to continue my life without having to be defensive.

A year later, in 1966, I entered the same competitions, and won them again. Although the competitive side of me was pleased this time I was more delighted on behalf of the Club. In some way I felt as if I been able to give something in return for all the value that I had received over the years.

Foreign Holiday

The Club used to arrange for a small group of senior boys to attend a camping holiday abroad once a year, and I attended in 1964 and 1966. Both these were visits to Sitges in Spain. In 1964 a group of eight of us loaded up the Club van with canoes, provisions and luggage, and drove down to Dover one Friday night in the middle of August to catch the ferry for Calais. Two days before Harry Roberts and his gang killed three policemen in Braybrook Road, Shepherds Bush. An event that shocked us all and occupied our discussion on the trip to Dover.

We landed in France during the late evening and Lew drove for a couple of hours before we stopped and caught some sleep in the van. We then spent all of Saturday and most of Sunday driving down to our campsite. Each of the boys had to take a spell of a couple of hours sitting next to Lew to ensure that he stayed awake. Like many Club events any health and safety officer would have been apoplectic at our conduct during these two weeks. But it did ensure that for a cost of £18 each of us could have their first holiday abroad.

I adored every moment of the trip but was shocked by many of the boys refusing to eat any of 'that foreign muck' and religiously eating steak and chips when we visited any restaurants. For most days, however, we cooked our own evening meal. Lew allocated responsibilities for preparing and cooking meals, as well as the more onerous washing up. About 4:00 p.m. most afternoons the boys would fill a large cooking dixie with the ingredients of what we called an Irish stew from different tins and spend an hour or so in the burning sun stirring the pot. After a couple of days, we would draw crowds wondering at our production of Mad Dogs and Englishmen.

After our evening meal we would assemble at a bar on site preparatory to our trip to town. I remember one evening sitting with a group of incredibly fit good-looking Scandinavians – all blonde and sun-tanned. One asked me what our intentions were. Having heard he looked at me with some amusement and said, 'But you are ugly, you will not pick up any girls.' He was so prosaic that I could not be offended. It was as if an adult had re-assured a child that the sky was blue, and the grass was green. His prediction was accurate. Now when I look at snapshots of that holiday and compare myself to my mates I do look like the runt of the litter. Ten and a half stone, all knees, cheek bones and elbows with an awful haircut.

On my second visit to Sitges in 1966 I was an experienced traveller but equally unsuccessful.

However, if there was one activity above all others that for me encapsulates Club life it was the Sunday morning canoeing trips on the Thames. We would start at 9:00 a.m., pack the van, and then drive down to Ravens Ait, Kingston on Thames. At the time it was an island predominantly used by sea scouts. We would unload, change and then canoe down to Hampton Court, have some sandwiches and then return. It was probably Lew's favourite sporting activity and there was always a wonderful sense of peace when we were on the water. We were miles away from Notting Dale.

10
Starting Out

While Lew and the Club were providing an escape route from domestic hell, my last two years at school provided the road to freedom. For some years I knew what I was rejecting but I was not sure what the replacement looked like. Although she had been mollified by the grant my mother's resentment could not be restrained. From this time onwards she would periodically accuse me of thinking that I was better than her, being 'stuck up', ignoring where I came from. I could only play classical music when she was out of the house. If I chose to watch a programme on television, then she would storm out. Quite clearly our tastes diverged, and for a while I flinched under the charge. I did feel disloyal. I felt really isolated between two worlds of the working class and the middle class. Lew was the only person who accepted me for who I was.

At school I chose the two subjects that I loved for 'A' levels, English and history, but really had no idea what I was letting myself in for. Our Fifth Form had contained about 30 boys, out of the 200 in my entry year. The Lower Sixth contained five boys only, four of us doing arts subjects and one doing science. We represented the academic success of the school after its first five years: it was a bleak outcome for all the hopes that had launched this new experiment in education. The school would eventually close in 1983, merging with Holland Park.

The positive side of being a small group meant that our teachers could offer us a level of teaching that would be enviable in a public school. The downside was that the rest of the school looked on us as aliens, beings that needed to be exterminated. My classmates received more of this hostility than me; partly because they lived on the periphery of the catchment area; partly because they were studiously anti-sports, and, not least, because they had no local affiliations. Although I was looked on as a poof, I got some mileage out of being an active member of the Harrow Boys Club and was known as a sportsman. I was still challenged and name-called on a regular basis, but I was not attacked on the streets around my home. In fact, I did act as a guide and protector when Jeff, a much bigger boy than me came weekly to my home in 1964 to watch the BBC2 series *The Great War*. I had to pick him up at Ladbroke Grove, walk him to my flat, and then complete the return journey. The idea that I was a protector was laughable, except that we did not laugh on any of those journeys. Luckily, my protection was not called on.

The change from 'O' to 'A' levels was dramatic. I had not liked the former method of study, nor the teachers much, and therefore, really came to loathe the English literature paper. For reasons I do not understand our English teacher at that level was someone training for the legal profession. He used to bring in copies of the magazines 'Reveille' and 'Titbits' and asked us to adopt their writing style. All essays needed a dramatic opening he would recommend. For example, 'When the submarine surfaced everyone on board was dead!' In addition, I was still struggling with maths and the teacher that I had attacked. Although we found a way of being in the same class, I still had to re-sit the 'O' level that autumn term.

However, as mature students we were responsible for planning and managing our own study, and simply had to present the requested number of essays on time. Learning suddenly acquired an exhilarating freedom, like stepping into a swimming pool. We also had several excellent teachers; Mr Stone and, Mr Dipstal, the deputy head, for English; and Brian Benjamin, our amazing history teacher who treated the four of us as adults. In addition, the London County Council provided us with weekly visits from the poet Martin Bell who opened the realms of modern poetry which was not on the syllabus. Very shyly, I showed him some of my early verses, and he recommended that I read Thomas Hardy, Edward Thomas and Louis MacNeice. The latter has remained an enduring find, and I would subsequently co-write his bibliography, which was published by Kaye and Ward in 1973.

Within a couple of weeks of the new syllabus I remember visiting Kensington Reference Library to read up on the early days of the French Revolution. As I sat in the reading room, with the evening darkness closing in, I looked up and experienced an intense feeling of wonder and gratitude for my luck. Not only was I choosing what to read and when, but I was also being asked to formulate and present my own view on the subject in the classroom. Up to then someone else was telling me what to think, or even worse, telling me not to think. Deliberation and questioning were not part of the Osborne tradition which insisted on compliance.

Even more radically, we began to study poetry, and I loved what I read. Just to mention the word would be enough to send Bill and Joe into a state of apoplexy. How on earth would that help me become a bugler in the Army? When I discovered that John Keats was the son of an innkeeper and was criticised severely for his presumption, I had found a role model. When I read the Blackwood Review which instructed him *'So back to the shop, Mr John, back to plasters, pills, and ointment boxes',* I could imagine his feelings. I had spent years hearing the same kind of nonsense. Both John and I knew what the world was really like.

I think that it was this kind of identification that allowed the internal mess and shame that I had felt to move aside. It never went away, just crawled up and hid inside like crab in a shell. I began to accommodate other possibilities in life. Creativity and imagination could take you to places and feelings that occupied other worlds. The dreary repetition of pointless behaviours and relationships was not inevitable. It was possible to find out and try new things.

In the wider world around me this message was being re-enforced in every way possible. Somewhere around 1963–4 colour started to seep into a black and white world that still seemed to be a stage set for a brief encounter. In a literal sense the introduction of Sunday colour supplements enabled everyone to see what was now available. Men were no longer restricted to wearing work suits that could have been in their dads' wardrobes. Fashion was aimed at people my age. The models looked like people that I knew rather than habitués of Knightsbridge. The cinema and theatre paraded people from my kind of background; Michael Caine, Terence Stamp, Albert Finney, David Bailey, Rita Tushingham and Twiggy. Social mobility was not just a possibility but a done deal. You could do and be what you wanted.

The repressive authority of the 1950s was being challenged through entertainment like *That Was the Week that Was* and *Beyond the Fringe*. The censorship battle over *Lady Chatterley's Lover* had been won, and by 1964 the Labour Party would replace a 13-year Conservative Government. The cliché about the 1960s is that if you remember it then you were not really there was a totally misleading idea. I was there and I remember it distinctly.

For some of my generation it may have been all about sex, drugs, and the rock and roll world, but I suspect that this was only for a few. Rock and roll had started in the late 1950s. I remember first hearing artists like Little Richard, Jerry Lee Lewis and Chuck Berry in the West Indian clubs of Ladbroke Grove. For years it remained the exclusive property of teenagers. Even when the white commercial world took over and began to make money and the original stars began to be replaced by the likes of Tommy Steele, Cliff Richard, and Pat Boone, it was still a minority interest.

When the Beatles really broke through in 1964, particularly in the USA, the music then became front page news. Within a couple of years pop and rock would become mainstream entertainment. But for me this was only part of the wider picture. Although I was a fan of Buddy Holly and then the Beatles, I was also listening to George Gershwin, Richard Rogers, Frank Sinatra, Al Jolson and Glenn Miller. I was also discovering Beethoven, Mozart and Dvorak. The real freedom was to find all that was available, and not to restrict choice for any reason. Why could I not like all these things?

During this period there was an acute generational gap between the baby boomers like me and our parents of the war generation. There was no clear defining moment somewhere between the Lady Chatterley ban and the Beatles first LP (Philip Larkin) when the world changed. A simple illustration of this can be seen in the TV and film coverage of the World Cup in 1966. The majority of the crowd were still dressed formally, wearing suits and ties, and the subsequent joy at winning was certainly confined. After the English team's triumphant appearance on the Kensington Park Hotel balcony the clamour quickly died down. Everyone went back to work and got on with their lives. This was one year before 'Sergeant Pepper' and the hippy revolution.

During the 'A' level years of 1964–65 I simply immersed myself in the arts and history as a traveller in a new land. What I did not realise until later was that I was a long way from home. Most of my contemporaries had left school at 15 and entered a world that excluded me. My family saw my education as further proof of my inherent badness; if I was of any worth, I should be out now supporting my mother. My teachers and Lew, my only adult contacts, were all middle class and very well-spoken. I was still struggling over the pronunciation of 'th' when reading out loud in class. In some ways all this contributed to a strong sense of alienation. There was no group that I could join or even vaguely identify with so my sense of shame would haunt me for many years.

Although I had always earned money from a range of part-time jobs from the age of 11 onwards, I was able to supplement my grant by working in a public library on Tuesday evening and Saturdays. The evening job was in Kensal Library, near Southam Street; on Saturdays I worked in Chelsea Library in Manresa Road. These represented the extremes social ends of the Royal Borough of Kensington and Chelsea, and symbolic of the split that I felt inside. However, the jobs encouraged me to apply for a full-time role when I left school. Although I was confident about good 'A' level results I had already decided that going to university was not a good choice, despite the active encouragement of my headmaster. I believed, with some justification at that stage university would exacerbate the internal split while what I really needed was simply to develop some social skills by working with normal people. I remember Brian Benjamin accusing me of being a conformist, but I do not think he appreciated the nature of the forces that I was dealing with. Middle class respectability, if that was my route, remained an outrageous goal.

It proved a fortuitous career choice. Not only did I have an enjoyable 10 years in public libraries, but in my first job at Brompton Road library I met the woman who would become my wife. Sylvia and I met in August 1965 and were married in January 1968. It would have been one year sooner, but I promised to help pay off the bills that my mother had developed over the years with credit companies. My reward for that extra year is that I had to try and mediate, almost daily, the continuing war between Elaine and my mother. Elaine had discovered boyfriends, and the joys of staying out late, all of which helped to fuel my mother's resentment about being a mother.

But at last, I married, and we moved to Southfields, the home of Wimbledon tennis. I had upset my mother by insisting that not one member of the Osborne family would be invited to the wedding. I had no desire to bring into my new life any of the pernicious relationships which had scarred the first twenty years of my life. If I had any sense, I would have excluded both her and my sister.

We rented a small first floor flat and began to establish our own life. We married on 28 January; four weeks later my mother and Elaine visited our new flat to give us news that I was to be an uncle. Elaine, at 18 years old, had beaten my mother in this race by two years. Their war had now found a new battlefield. Elaine had a son and my mother a grandson. The continuing battle over 'who was the real mother?' was about to begin. Within three years we moved to the West Midlands, and after eight years there it was on to Horsham in West Sussex. I believed that all was now behind me. By geography I had exorcised my past and I could now keep it at a distance.

11
And So

And so, why do I feel the need to write down the details of this unbalanced childhood 50 odd years after the events described. I have lived a happy and fulfilling life with my wife and three children.

Well, the real story is often the one that starts when the final page closes. When the hero walks off into the sunset after the battle ends. I thought that I was now free and put my past behind me. True, the sounds of battle could be heard off stage, but I believed that I had both an emotional as well as a physical distance from the antagonists.

In the early 1970s Elaine met and married a much older man, whom my mother hated. To be fair, the chances of Elaine finding one that my mother would not hate was probably very slim. Despite the mutual hatred encompassing all three of them they stayed locked in contact and combat. In addition to the periodic rows with her sisters she felt able to take on this additional chore. During these years my mother was most insistent that Elaine and I should stay in contact and tried on several occasions to engineer a meeting. In response I met Elaine twice, both times confirming the soundness of my original choice.

A major crisis in their own relationship occurred in the late 1980s when my mother retired from work. Elaine and her husband ran into financial difficulties with a grocer's shop that they were running in Buckinghamshire. In addition to going to stay with them, my mother volunteered the whole of her pension pot to the pair to help with their debts. A few years before she retired Mum found a full-time job with Shell and was able to save some money. Her offer to help was a clear sign of madness. The money went and was never paid back. The first I knew of this event was a telephone call from my mother crying about her lack of money and her inability to manage on her pension. This was clearly an excuse to tell me the story of Elaine's duplicity. When I confronted my sister about this 'loan' she said that she always expected me to support my mother, so she never considered paying it back. For her, there was no issue. Her family must come first.

Accordingly, I gave my mother money to redress the problem, and I felt some relief when Elaine and her husband moved to the USA. Her son had moved there some years before. Even after this departure my mother was unwilling to let go of her daughter. Long argumentative phone calls were punctuated by a couple of trips to the states. On her last visit she spent two weeks with them and paid out $2,000 for the privilege of picking up the bills for three people. When I confronted her about this, she said that paying was easier than having a row every day. However, this did not stop her moaning about how badly she had been abused.

During the same period, she started a relationship with her last boyfriend, Johnny, whom she had successfully taken away from her widowed sister, Lizzie. Johnny continued my mother's rich tradition of boyfriends. He was a drunk, unreliable, and was kept in bed and lodging while maintaining his own home elsewhere. Every time we spoke, she would complain about him to Sylvia and myself then immediately tell us not to say a word about it to him. I never responded to any of these invitations. Never again would I interfere in her love life.

During these years, I really believed that I had exorcised my past and was managing my mother. I thought I knew who she was and what she was capable of but felt I was above the fray. Astutely, she never attempted to interfere in my relationship with Sylvia and the children. She knew that would have ended our relationship on the spot. Over the years we would take her on summer holidays with us, although it was clear to all of us that she never really enjoyed being away from her comfort zone. We picked up the same level of discomfort when she stayed at our homes over the years. It seemed that if she was not in control of the situation then she found it difficult to cope. On a couple of occasions, she manufactured a row to leave early.

As she grew older, I began to look on her as an old lady who had suffered a miserable life and felt concerned enough to make her last year's relatively stress free. I had long ago given up the idea, if I ever had one, that this was my mother. Of course, that was a biological fact but that was about as maternal as it would ever get.

In my late twenties I wrote the following, not about us, but describing a contemporary of mine who lived with his mother. Hence the use of the third party.

Sons and Mothers

His mother loves him
With a love she gives to cats and choirboys.
He loves his mother
With a love he gives for a fireside at evening.
Chocolates, fruits and nuts upon the table
And the television on.
She admires the boy who continues at his job.
He admires the mother who kept him for so long.

The house is regulated,
Each room is stamped with signs of his and hers.
There is no opportunity for outside interference,
They seal their property and ears with wax.
He ignores the wayward voices.
She enjoys idyllic comfort that must end
For him but not for her.
He is the one that must live after her.
She is the one that lived before he came.

Men she has decided are after just one thing.
Girls he has decided are after just one thing.
Across the table they watch each other,
They do not speak but are contented.
Chocolates, flowers, fruits and nuts,
Silence at the fireside,
Mutual admiration,
Suspended animation.

And Dad is buried in the garden.

In retrospect, of course, I recognise now that the state of suspended animation was the simple fact that we never spoke about the past. I, initially, because I was fed up with the Catherine Cookson mythology; then secondly, because I simply lost interest. She would only talk about certain episodes which involved not understanding the behaviour of her sisters and her daughter.

What makes my sense of distance so bizarre, is that I trained as a therapist in my thirties. An essential part of that training is that the therapist must spend at least one year as a patient, and then subsequently attend refresher sessions. The aims of this are to understand the relationship from the patient's side as well as to deal with any issues that might affect you as a therapist. During my training, the issues about staying with Bill and Ivy emerged, as did the lack of feelings for my missing father, but the 'state of suspended animation' was never breached. As a patient I had no inhibition about dealing with things that caused me problems, so this was not a problem of reluctance. I genuinely believed that it was all behind me. I also realised that I could never share my anger or resentment about those years with her. I believed that it would be cruel to tell her what I thought about her and what she allowed to happen to me as a child. Not even I could give an old lady a bad time. What would be the point?

Near the end of her life my mother would occasionally start a conversation with Sylvia about her childhood or the 'true' love of her life, Earl Clark. Sylvia would then tell me things that were either new to me or contradicted the stories that I had been told as a child. My mother would unload tirades against Elaine, but I simply agreed with whatever was said.

My illusions started to fracture in the last six years of her life. It started with a phone call from one of her neighbours. We were now living at Bexleyheath, winding down to my retirement. My mother had been rushed to hospital after the police had broken down her flat door. She was near death in a central London hospital suffering from a severe bladder infection and dehydration. I rushed straight across and had an anxious wait until the doctors explained that her state had now normalised. However, she spent a long time in hospital, and then time in a nursing home so that she could be trained to walk again. This period of nine months was dramatic but not unexpected for someone in her eighties. However, this remained a pattern for the rest of her life. Firstly, she would develop an infection by not eating, drinking, and taking her medicine. She would then retire to bed and not answer her phone or the front door. Until a kindly neighbour took possession of a duplicate door key, her door would be broken down, an ambulance called, and a long hospital stay ensued. On each occasion my family and I would make many long journeys to hospital until she improved. On each return home she would promise faithfully to drink, eat, and take her medicine. These promises quickly expired. For the first five years she spent at least half that time in hospital. In 2013, the last nine months of her life, she spent about six to seven months in various hospitals, and averaged an emergency call out monthly. On at least three occasions in the six years the doctors warned me that she was close to death. However, there was also a reversion to the behaviour that she used when I was a child. On several occasions I was phoned by hospitals to say that she was abusive and uncooperative. They believed her behaviour to be a symptom of old age and her illness. They would ask me to come and talk to her in the belief that she would respond to her son. One November night I was called to St Mary's Hospital in Paddington because she was sitting rocking on her bed, saying over and over, 'I want to go home!' She was still suffering from an infection, wearing her nightie, while the incessant rain ran down the windows. When I refused to call a taxi and take her home, she started abusing me and shouting that she never wanted to see me again. I walked out of the hospital and caught a train back to Bexleyheath. Some days later she rang me to apologise for her behaviour. She must have felt desperate because it was the only time in my life that she apologised for anything.

A few months later when my sons turned up at her hospital bedside, she was incredibly rude to them and accusing us of not caring for her. This time I went to the hospital and told her that should she ever talk to my kids again in that way then she would be on her own. That was when I received my second and last apology.

All these six years were incredibly wearing both physically and emotionally. Any day could be her last. In June 2013 she said that she wanted to be moved from London, nearer to where we lived in Broadstairs. Knowing that she had lived all her life in Notting Dale I was very dubious and talked with her about what such a move could mean. I explained that by giving up her flat she would not be able to return. I attended two case conferences with her and her social worker about a proposed move and they both agreed that this was the right thing. Having spent a good part of the last two years travelling to central London hospitals, listening to her endless complaints about the way they had treated her, and how lonely she felt in her London flat, I finally agreed.

I arranged for her to move into a wonderful home in Broadstairs 15 minutes' walk from our house, where she had an en-suite bedroom with lunch and dinner cooked and served to her daily. I undertook endless arrangements to make this happen and completed the move in September. For the first three weeks all seemed to be well. Then again, she stopped eating, drinking, and taking her medicine. Not surprisingly she took to her bed again and the home was thrown into a panic because they were not a nursing institution. They had never had to cope with such an inmate. She started to complain about the home, Broadstairs, and the fact that she had left all her friends back in London. The reality of course was that her friends had died many years before and she had become totally dependent on one person to look after her, do her shopping, and run her errands. My mother then demanded that I move her back into the flat that she had vacated in London. When I pointed out that this was no longer possible, she stated that she would crawl back to London on her hands and knees if necessary and find herself a flat. I refused of course, we rowed, and then she told me that she wanted nothing more to do with me.

The staff in the home, the local doctor, like all the helping professions before them, assumed that her behaviour was a by-product of her illness or a consequence of her age. They also assumed that I had some ability to influence her. The truth was that my mother was simply behaving in the way that she had when I was a child. When she wanted anything, no matter how unreasonable, it had to be delivered here and now, otherwise everyone would suffer. Her health and general condition deteriorated alarmingly, and she lost four stone in weight. It was clear to all that she was dying. Just as it got to the point when the home was telling me that she had to be moved because she needed 24-hour nursing care she was taken into hospital. She even refused to go to the hospital and tried to bite the ambulance assistants as they moved her from her bed.

Once in hospital she refused to eat, drink, or take medicine. When the staff explained the situation about the impossibility of a return to London she moaned and whined, refused co-operation and started to offer dramatic performances to all and sundry. One day she would be shouting out she wanted to go home; the next she would be crying out to her dad (of all people!) to come and fetch her, and the next she would simply lie there and refuse to talk. The stone face with the head tilted away from you was her default position, one that I had seen too many times. Sylvia and I would turn up each day not knowing what to expect. The most amazing episode of all came near the end of her hospital stay when breaking one of her stony silences she suddenly said, 'I love you, Neil, and always have.' Sylvia and I looked at each other in amazement. That was the only time in my life I heard her use the word 'love' in any context about any person, let alone me.

Within a couple of weeks, the hospital said that they could do no more for her and recommended that she enter a hospice. She was therefore moved. Here again she refused to co-operate with the staff. They, like all previous helpers merely treated this as a symptom of her decline. The last day that I saw her, Monday, 11 November, she complained that a catheter was not working and that I ought to get a nurse. The nurses were busy on an emergency in another room. While she was waiting, she uttered her last words to me, “If you can’t help me then you might as well bugger off home!” In some ways this was the most fitting epitaph to our relationship. I went onto the lounge of the home while the problem was sorted. I did not return to the room. So those were her last words to me.

I decided not to visit her on the Tuesday. I needed a break. At 9:00 p.m. that evening I received a telephone call that said, ‘Your mum died ten minutes ago. She died peacefully.’ I put the phone down and felt a sense of massive relief.

During these last weeks, the strain of dealing with her had led me to talk to the vicar of my church. In simple terms, I was finding it difficult to follow a basic Christian command to honour your father and mother. He was supportive and suggested that I stopped attending church for a couple of weeks because other members of the congregation through their concern might add to my troubles. The guilt of accepting that I had no love for my mother even though she was dying was a corrosive feeling.

I had arranged with the vicar that I wanted to speak the 23rd psalm at my mother’s funeral. I wanted to offer something in recognition of her life. When we arrived at the crematorium the sight of my mother’s coffin made me feel giddy and sick. At the appropriate time I went to the front and began to read. ‘The Lord is my shepherd…’ at this point I broke down, sobbing convulsively. It took me ages to complete the reading. I still have no idea of who or what I was crying for. My mother? Myself?

The woman that I had called Mum for 66 years was gone. She had given birth to me but that was about the last time that we were close. Her life was now over, and I could not identify one time in her life when she was happy or was able to enjoy anything about her. Somehow or the other she was impervious to happiness or enjoyment. Life was something that had to be endured on her terms. I remembered one time in hospital when an examining doctor asked her questions about her condition. According to my mother, she was eating, drinking, and taking her medicine, and all was well. When the doctor left, I asked her why she had lied to him. She said, 'You have to tell these people what they want to hear.' When I explained that she was only damaging herself she put on her stone face and turned her head away from me. This conversation was now over.

Her last wishes were carried out and after cremation her ashes were scattered at sea. She had specified this request in the last revision of her will.

Why? I have no idea. Luckily, the undertakers were able to make suitable arrangements. When all was ready, they asked me if I wanted to attend. I said no. I just wanted to let go. All this was now over.

The stresses of her last three months were overwhelming. At the age of 67 I felt on the edge of a nervous breakdown. My doctor prescribed sedatives in the short term but also recommended that I have some sessions with a counsellor. I found the sessions helpful, and by the end of January 2014 I was calming down. At my third and final session, the counsellor offered a simple observation. I was dealing with a special kind of grief. I was not grieving for my mother but for a lost childhood. She offered to help me work through this loss, but my understanding was enough. I never had a childhood, never once felt loved, cared for, or even safe.

As the weeks turned into months, I tried to make some sense of what had happened. I had allowed myself to become a victim and that I hated. Events had proved that I did not have sufficient resources to cope. After surviving all that my childhood had thrown at me, I had crumbled to an old dying woman.

At the age of five I knew that I was being systematically persecuted by Bill and Ivy. I had found a way to respond. I decided that they were crazy, and I was not. As a result, I began to recognise the sadness and futility of their lives. Even then, they were the victims and not me. But I had adopted a carapace of numbness. That had now broken open.

At the age of 15 when the roof fell in with the death of John Michael, I chose to punish others, and ultimately, then myself. It was not a good choice, but I did not break. True, I discovered depths of shame and remorse. These feelings never went away, at best I was able to sublimate or simply ignore them. It meant that I lacked confidence and automatically assumed when things went wrong that, at the very least, I had a share of the responsibility.

In retrospect, the worst choice I made was not to end my relationship with my mother when I married. I had ended my relationship with the rest of my family at that time. Not because of her or her behaviour but because whatever I tried to do for her was an utter waste of time. All my childhood experiences had proved this to be the truth. I have a simple example of what I mean from the final years.

During our first summer in Broadstairs after I retired, I wheeled her in a push chair down to the pier on a sunny August afternoon. I positioned her chair so that she could look across Viking Bay towards the bandstand. All around were holidaymakers on the sand playing, swimming or sunbathing. The sea sparkled in the sun, and the sea gulls swooped and soared across the sky. We had just come from lunch and an afternoon of peace and enjoyment awaited. This was a place that we both had good memories of from holidays 60 years before. Once I made sure that she was comfortable I said, 'What a beautiful day!'

There was no response, so I turned myself to look her in the face, and repeated, 'What a beautiful day!' She said, 'Yes.' But her face was carved in stone, and her voice was level and flat. We then stood in silence for about 30 minutes before I wheeled her chair back home. She had no idea of what I was talking about. She had no interest in Broadstairs, her past, or me. Inside, she had been dead for far too many years.

I eventually found a way to let go. I remembered one of her last days in the hospital when a storm was raging outside, and rain was pouring down the windows. It reminded me of a time in Wornington Road, probably my earliest memory. I had sat and watched the rain streaming across the windows. I was as alone then as I was now sitting by her bed. But this was the end.

Breaking Point

I watch the nurses move across the floor,
Calmly, smoothly, responding to your call.
They offer kindness then softly close the door.
I sit beside your bed, alert to all.
The struggles that contort your hands and face,
Tired, waiting for an end so long delayed,
I have a silent role in this antiseptic place,
Not quite an end more an endless fade.

I hope you find the peace that death will bring.
For at the end, you keep the world at bay,
To nurse your still-born child of suffering.
This close to death there's nothing more to say.
Beyond the glass, a bird with tired wing,
Caught by the storm is simply blown away.

What I needed to recall was that I had survived, I had not been blown away, I had endured.

In fact, there were many pleasures and enjoyments that had and still enrich my life. And then I remembered an episode with Lew near the end of his life. He was walking with difficulty using a stick. His legs were black with deep vein thrombosis. He had recently suffered a heart attack and had also been told that he had inoperable prostate cancer. We were sitting in a National Trust shop in Runnymede just starting on an afternoon cream tea. As he put down his buttered scone Lew looked up, eyes sparkling, and said,

'My, stars and garters, how lovely.' Sylvia and I burst out laughing at his joy, and his capacity to share that with others.

I also remembered the last time I saw him alive in Reading hospital, about three days before the end. I left his bedside and stood in the carpark that Sunday morning needing to cry before I could safely drive my car. I was there for about 20 minutes. But when I attended both his funeral and a subsequent memorial service at Windsor Castle I did not cry. My heart was full of the joy that we had shared over the years. Whatever problems we face, as we all do, without joy there is little purpose.

My story is about two people, complete contrasts. One was anti-life who survived for 86 years in a dark, dark world. The other was a man who gave himself to others and helped life grow.

When I die, and if I am lucky enough to get to heaven, the gate may well be opened by St Peter or some other dignitary. What I do know, however, is that Lew will be standing just on the inside of the gate, next to a large notice board covered with details of forthcoming events.

Although my journey to heaven may have been taxing and I enter tired and weary he will smile and say, 'Good evening, Sunshine! There is a cross-country race this weekend on Dartmoor; and I am also looking for a team, the following day, to take part in a canoe race down the Wye Valley. Can I put your name down for both events?'

And I will smile and say, 'I'll be delighted.' And I will be. Because I always was.